SOUPED
UP

SOUPED UP

**DELICIOUSLY
NUTRITIOUS RECIPES
FOR SATISFYING
HOMEMADE SOUPS**

RYLAND PETERS & SMALL
LONDON • NEW YORK

Senior Designer Toni Kay
Editors Miriam Catley & Lesley Malkin
Production Patricia Harrington
Art Director Leslie Harrington
Editorial Director Julia Charles
Publisher Cindy Richards
Indexer Hilary Bird

First published in 2018 by
Ryland Peters & Small
20–21 Jockey's Fields, London
WC1R 4BW
and
341 E 116th St, New York NY 10029
www.rylandpeters.com

10 9 8 7 6 5 4 3

Recipe collection compiled by
Miriam Catley.

ISBN: 978-1-78879-034-5

Printed in China

A CIP record for this book is available
from the British Library.

US Library of Congress Cataloging-in-
Publication Data has been applied for.

NOTES:
• Both British (Metric) and American
(Imperial plus US cups) measurements
are included in these recipes for your
convenience, however it is important
to work with one set of measurements
and not alternate between the two
within a recipe.
• All spoon measurements are level
unless otherwise specified.
• All eggs are medium (UK) or large (US),
unless specified as large, in which case
US extra-large should be used. Uncooked
or partially cooked eggs should not
be served to the very old, frail, young
children, pregnant women or those with
compromised immune systems.
• Ovens should be preheated to the
specified temperatures. We recommend
using an oven thermometer. If using a
fan-assisted oven, adjust temperatures
according to the manufacturer's
instructions.
• When a recipe calls for the grated
zest of citrus fruit, buy unwaxed fruit
and wash well before using. If you can
only find treated fruit, scrub well in
warm soapy water before using.

CONTENTS

INTRODUCTION   6

BASIC STOCKS   8

SMOOTH SOUPS   10

LIGHT SOUPS   46

HEARTY SOUPS   76

LUXURIOUS SOUPS   112

INDEX   142

CREDITS   144

INTRODUCTION

There's nothing more comforting and soothing than a bowl of soup. Whether you're looking for a way to use a glut of seasonal produce, increase your daily intake of fresh vegetables, or you simply crave the comfort only a bowlful of soup can bring, this book of tempting recipes is for you. Simple to make, easy to serve and full of flavour and texture possibilities, soup is a great way to eat any time of the day, from a light lunch to a satisfying supper, plus it's a surefire way to ensure you get all the nourishment you need with the minimum of fuss in the kitchen and at the table.

Soups are always useful for anyone managing a family budget but also make the perfect solution when you are cooking for just one or two people. Most of the recipes in this book will freeze well (just avoid freezing those made with dairy products or seafood) and lend themselves to batch cooking. Simply store your freshly made and cooled soup in sealable freezerproof containers in portion sizes that suit you. That way a quick and sustaining after-work supper is always to hand, or that unexpected hungry crowd can be fed a welcome hot meal from a simmering pot on the stovetop.

Here you'll find ideas to suit every taste and style of occasion with recipes, both classic and modern, collected from all around the globe. Soup can be enjoyed hot or cold, be warming or refreshing, light or rich, rustic or elegant. Ideas for summer include uplifting ingredients such as asparagus, fennel, peas and watercress, seasoned with tangy citrus and garnished with créme fraîche and snipped green herbs. Heartier recipes to sustain you on a cold winter's day are rich with starchy root vegetables, pulses, beans and hints of warm spice and served with a swirl of cream and a melting grilled cheese. Equiped with a good sharp knife, a large saucepan, a ladle and this book a delicious meal in a bowl is just a chop and a slow simmer away!

BASIC STOCKS

'Stock' forms the basis of soup and while there are some good powdered or compound stocks available it is well worth taking the time to make your own. You can make it when you have a little time available or appropriate ingredients to hand and pop it in the freezer for later use. If using homemade simply isn't an option, try to use a bought one with as few artificial additives as possible or your delicious soup could end up tasting like a poor packeted relation.

VEGETABLE STOCK

2 onions, halved

2 leek, thickly sliced

1 fennel bulb, halved

4 celery sticks, thickly sliced

4 carrots, peeled and thickly sliced

1–2 bay leaves

a few sprigs of fresh thyme

a small bunch of fresh parsley

10 white peppercorns

sea salt

MAKES ABOUT 1.5 LITRES/6 CUPS

Put all ingredients in a large saucepan and top up with 2.5 litres/quarts water. Cover the pan with a lid, bring the liquid to a simmer. Let it simmer for 1½ hours, removing the lid for the last 30 minutes so it can reduce a little. Pass the stock through a sieve/strainer and discard the solids. Adjust the seasoning with salt and use as per the recipe.

Tip If you prefer a slightly richer flavour, brown the vegetables in a tablespoon of butter before adding the liquid to the pan.

FISH STOCK

50 g/3½ tablespoons butter

2 garlic cloves

12 shallots, peeled

1 leek, thickly sliced

2 kg/4½ lbs. white fish carcass/bones (not oily fish or salmon), heads and all but no guts

4 celery sticks, thickly sliced

½ fennel bulb, halved

2 carrots, peeled and thickly sliced

a large bunch of fresh tarragon

a large bunch of fresh parsley

10 peppercorns

sea salt

MAKES ABOUT 1.5 LITRES/6 CUPS

Melt the butter in a large saucepan and add the garlic, shallots and leek. Cook for a few minutes until softened, then add fish to the pan. Top up with 2 litres/quarts water. Add the celery, fennel, carrots, herbs and peppercorns, cover with the lid and simmer very gently for about an hour, removing the lid for the last 20 minutes so that it can reduce a little. Pass the stock through a sieve/strainer and discard the solids. Adjust the seasoning with salt and use as per the recipe.

BEEF STOCK

3 kg/6½ lbs. beef bones
2 carrots, peeled and thickly sliced
1 onion, halved
3 celery sticks, thickly sliced
2 leeks, thickly sliced
1 bay leaf
a large bunch of fresh parsley
a few sprigs of fresh thyme
10 black peppercorns
sea salt

MAKES ABOUT 1 LITRE/4 CUPS

Preheat the oven to 200°C (400°F) Gas 6.

Put the beef bones in a roasting pan and roast them in the preheated oven for about 30 minutes to give colour and depth of flavour. Transfer the bones to a stock pan. Deglaze the roasting pan by pouring a little hot water into the pan to pick up any juices that are stuck to the pan (so no flavour is left behind!), then pour into the stock pan with the bones. Add all vegetables, herbs and seasonings to the pan and top with 4 litres/quarts water. Cover the pan with a lid and bring to a simmer. Let simmer very slowly for hours and hours – the more the better and no less than 5 hours! Pass the stock through a sieve/strainer and discard the solids. Transfer the stock to a clean pan, return to the heat and cook, uncovered, until reduced to 1 litre/4 cups – this will intensify the stock's flavour. Adjust the seasoning with salt, and use as per the recipe.

Tip Ask the butcher for marrow bones, as these will give the best jellied result. You know you have a good stock if it sets hard when cooled.

CHICKEN STOCK

25 g/2 tablespoons butter, or vegetable or olive oil
4 kg/8¾ lbs. chicken wings or a chicken carcass
2 onions, halved
1 leek, thickly sliced
2 garlic cloves
2 celery sticks, thickly sliced
200 g/7 oz. button mushrooms, halved
2 carrots, peeled and thickly sliced
a mix of fresh herbs, such as bay leaves, tarragon, parsley, chervil, thyme (for a very plain stock, use parsley only)
20 black peppercorns
sea salt

MAKES ABOUT 1.5 LITRES/6 CUPS

Heat the butter or oil in a large saucepan and add the chicken. Cook for a few minutes in the butter, without colouring, then add the onion, leek and garlic and cook until softened. Add all other vegetables to the pan and pour over 3 litres/quarts water. Add the fresh herbs and the peppercorns, cover the pan and bring to a simmer. Let the stock simmer for 1½ hours, removing the lid for the last 30 minutes so that it can reduce a little. Pass the stock through a fine-mesh sieve/strainer and discard the solids. Skim the stock, if necessary. Adjust the seasoning with salt, and use as per the recipe.

SMOOTH SOUPS

MUSHROOM SOUP WITH GARLIC CROUTONS

There is something very comforting about a good mushroom soup, with its particular earthy flavour and smooth richness. Here, garlicky croutons and freshly fried chestnut/cremini mushrooms are a simple but effective way of addding flavour and texture boost to this classic soup.

2 tablespoons sunflower oil

½ onion, chopped

1 leek, finely chopped

a sprig of thyme, leaves only

500 g/1 lb. field mushrooms, stalks trimmed and chopped

1 potato, peeled and diced

a splash of Maderia or Amontillado sherry

700 ml/3 cups good chicken stock (see page 9)

freshly ground nutmeg

sea salt and freshly ground black pepper

1 tablespoon olive oil

200 g/6½ oz. chestnut/cremini mushrooms, sliced, to serve

double/heavy cream, to garnish

freshly chopped chives, to garnish

GARLIC CROUTONS

2 tablespoons olive oil

1 garlic clove, peeled

2 slices of day-old rustic bread, crusts trimmed off, cut into small cubes

SERVES 4

Heat the sunflower oil in a large saucepan over a medium heat. Add the onion, leek and thyme leaves and fry gently, stirring now and then, for 5 minutes until softened. Add the field mushrooms and fry, stirring, for 3 minutes until lightly browned.

Mix in the diced potato, then add the Madeira or sherry and cook, stirring, for a minute. Pour in the chicken stock and bring to the boil. Reduce the heat, cover and simmer for 25 minutes.

Meanwhile, make the croutons. Heat the olive oil in a frying pan/skillet over a medium heat. Add the garlic clove and fry briefly until fragrant. Add the cubes of bread and fry until golden-brown and crisp, discarding the garlic clove when it browns.

Purée the cooked soup until smooth in a food processor or using a stick blender. Season with salt, freshly ground pepper and nutmeg. Bring to a simmer again in the pan to heat through.

When ready to serve, heat 1 tablespoon of olive oil in a frying pan/skillet over a medium-high heat. Fry the chestnut/cremini mushrooms until lightly browned.

Serve the warm soup in bowls, garnished with a swirl of double/heavy cream, some hot fried mushrooms, garlic croutons and chopped chives.

CREAM OF CELERIAC & WHITE BEAN SOUP
WITH TOASTED HAZELNUTS & TRUFFLE OIL

Visually honest soups are intriguing: when you taste them it's almost like a game of 'what is that flavour coming through?' This is one of those soups. Here, the ugly brute that is celeriac has such a wonderful nutty sweetness, while the starch from the smooth white beans gives the soup richness, and the hazelnuts and truffle oil work to bring both texture and forest-floor flavours.

150 g/1 cup hazelnuts

90 ml/6 tablespoons olive oil

8 banana shallots, finely diced

2 garlic cloves, roughly chopped

2 celeriac/celery root, peeled and diced

2 celery sticks, sliced

2 bay leaves

2 litres/quarts chicken stock (see page 9)

a 400-g/14-oz. can cannellini beans, drained

180 ml/¾ cup double/ heavy cream

a squeeze of lemon juice, to taste

sea salt and ground black pepper

truffle oil, for drizzling

SERVES 6-8

To toast the hazelnuts, put them in a roasting pan and pop them in a medium–hot oven for about 10 minutes, until they are just golden and smelling lovely. Tip the toasted nuts into a kitchen cloth and rub well to remove the skins, then roughly chop them.

Put the olive oil, shallots, garlic, celeriac/celery root, celery and bay leaves in a saucepan and toss over medium—high heat for a few minutes, until beginning to soften. Add the stock to the pan along with three-quarters of the toasted hazelnuts and the cannellini beans. Cover the pan and simmer gently for about 15–20 minutes, until the celeriac/celery root is very tender. Draw the pan off the heat and remove the bay leaves.

With a stick blender, whizz the soup until very smooth, then stir in the cream and blend briefly again until well mixed. If you think the soup is a little thin, allow to simmer gently over very low heat to reduce down a little – this should be a smooth, velvety soup. When you are happy with the consistency, season with salt and pepper and lift the flavour with a squeeze of lemon juice.

Ladle the soup into bowls, scatter the reserved chopped hazelnuts over the top and drizzle with truffle oil to serve.

ROASTED TOMATO SOUP WITH RAREBIT TOASTS

The tomato is held in high regard in the Mediterranean countries, where a second-rate tomato is simply not an option! Many dishes that feature them have few other ingredients, so it's essential that the tomatoes themselves taste good. Dishes such as Spanish salmorejo, a cold tomato and bread soup, are dependent on the tastiest of the summer crop. To be assured of their quality, buy your tomatoes from a farmers' market in summer if you can.

1 kg/2¼ lbs. Italian tomatoes, such as Roma, halved

2 small red onions, quartered

6 sprigs of fresh lemon thyme

1 teaspoon white sugar

1 teaspoon sea salt

2 garlic cloves, sliced

2 tablespoons olive oil

500 ml/2 cups Vegetable Stock (see page 8)

sea salt and freshly ground black pepper

RAREBIT TOAST FINGERS

100 g/4 oz. Cheddar cheese

3 tablespoons wheat beer

1 tablespoon Worcestershire sauce

4 slices of wholemeal/whole-wheat bread or baguette

SERVES 4

Preheat the oven to 170°C (325°F) Gas 3. Put the tomatoes, onion, lemon thyme, sugar, salt, garlic and oil in a large bowl. Use your hands to toss the ingredients to combine and evenly coat them in the oil. Tip the mixture out onto a baking sheet and roast in the preheated oven for 1½ hours. Discard the lemon thyme sprigs then put the tomatoes, onions and any tasty juices in a food processor or blender and process until smooth, adding a little stock if the mixture is too thick to process. Transfer to a large saucepan, add the stock and cook over gentle heat for 10 minutes. Season to taste and keep warm.

Preheat the grill/broiler to high. Put the Cheddar, beer and Worcestershire sauce in a small saucepan set over low heat. Stir until the cheese has melted and the mixture is smooth. Toast the bread under the preheated grill/broiler on one side only. Spread about 2 tablespoons of the cheese mixture on each untoasted side of bread and grill/broil until it is bubbling and golden. Cut into fingers and serve with the soup.

FRESH SILKY SEASONAL ASPARAGUS SOUP
WITH SOUR CREAM & CHIVES

Asparagus represents a big investment of a gardener's time, but the result is worth every moment, as few vegetables can 'stand alone' in the kitchen the way asparagus can. This silky smooth, velvety asparagus soup is simple, elegant and perfect for any occasion. It's great served with a little sprinkle of chive flower petals, if you have them in your garden. The subtle purple mimic's the asparagus tips – so elegant and so delicious.

50 g/3½ tablespoons butter

6 banana (or other sweet) shallots, diced

8 new potatoes, peeled and diced

1½ bunches of asparagus spears

800 ml/3⅓ cups Vegetable or Chicken Stock (see pages 8–9)

100 ml/7 tablespoons double/ heavy cream and sour cream combined (for a little more 'edge' use all sour cream, or for a richer soup use all double/heavy cream)

sea salt and ground black pepper

freshly snipped chives, to serve

SERVES 4–6

Melt the butter in a large saucepan and add the shallots and potatoes. Toss them in the butter and cook very gently so that they take in some of the butter, but do not allow them to colour. Pour over the stock, cover and simmer for about 15 minutes, until the potatoes are tender.

Snap the woody ends off the asparagus spears. (Breaking them at the point at which they are naturally inclined to snap means you remove any woody, fibrous stalk, which is not good for the soup.) Roughly chop the spears and add them to the pan with the potatoes and stock. Cook for only a few more minutes, as you want to keep the vibrant green. When the asparagus is almost tender, draw the pan off the heat and blend the soup with a stick blender, adding the cream a little at a time as you blend, as this will help give the soup a silky finish. Season to taste with salt and freshly ground black pepper.

Ladle the soup into smart white bowls, garnish with freshly snipped chives and serve immediately.

PURPLE SPROUTING BROCCOLI SOUP
WITH BLUE CHEESE

The colour and flavour of the purple sprouting variety of broccoli is superior and more intense than its more common workaday green cousin, so it is ideal for making into soup when in season. A soft blue cheese complements the soup perfectly, but choose one that is not too strongly flavoured.

50 g/3½ tablespoons salted butter

6 banana shallots, finely chopped

3 potatoes, peeled and diced

4 celery sticks, sliced

1.5 litres/6 cups chicken stock (see page 9)

950 g/2 lbs. 2 oz. purple sprouting or new-season tender broccoli

400 g/14 oz. creamy blue cheese, such as Stilton

a pinch of grated nutmeg

200 ml/¾ cup double/heavy cream

ground black pepper

croutons, to serve

SERVES 6

Melt the butter in a large saucepan, add the shallots and cook gently for a few minutes to soften. Add the potato and celery, and stir to coat well with the butter. Add the stock and bring the liquid to the boil, then simmer for 15–20 minutes, until the potato is almost tender. Add the broccoli and continue to cook for a further 3–5 minutes, until the stalks are tender. It is crucial not to overcook the broccoli or you lose the lovely bright colour. Purée the soup immediately with a blender. When smooth, crumble in three quarters of the blue cheese and add a pinch of nutmeg and a good twist of black pepper, to season. (The cheese can be quite salty, so you probably won't need salt, too.) Stir in almost all of the cream, reserving a little to garnish.

Ladle the soup into bowls, garnish with a swirl of cream and crumble over the remaining blue cheese. Serve piping hot as quickly as possible, with croutons.

CARROT & FENNEL SOUP
WITH FRESH LEMON, DILL & NIGELLA SEED

This soup was inspired by summer in Provence, where there is an abundance of fresh ingredients filled with Provençal sunshine. You too can capture the essence of that wonderful place in this lively soup, which is quietly sophisticated. A dramatic fleck of black nigella and olives against the vibrant yellow of the base, the lovely hint of aniseed/anise from the fennel and the tanginess of fresh lemon all work together so well.

2 tablespoons extra virgin olive oil, plus extra for drizzling

1 onion, diced

2 garlic cloves, crushed

4 carrots, peeled and diced

½ butternut (or other brightly-fleshed) squash, peeled, deseeded and diced

½ fennel bulb, roughly chopped

800 ml/3⅓ cups Vegetable Stock (see page 8)

a small bunch of fresh dill, roughly chopped

120 ml/½ cup crème fraîche or plain yogurt

freshly grated zest and freshly squeezed juice of 1 lemon

½ teaspoon nigella seeds (black onion seeds), plus a few extra to garnish

sea salt and ground black pepper

a few very good black olives, finely chopped, to garnish

SERVES 4–6

Heat the olive oil in a large saucepan and add the onion, garlic, carrots and squash. Toss over high heat until all the vegetables are beginning to soften at the edges. Add the fennel and stock and simmer for about 20 minutes, until the vegetables are tender. Draw the pan off the heat and stir in the fresh dill. Whizz the soup with a stick blender until very smooth. Stir in the crème fraîche and lemon zest and juice, then sprinkle in the nigella seeds. Finally, season to taste.

Serve the soup hot or cold with a scatter of chopped black olives and a few more nigella seeds, and a drizzle of extra virgin olive oil, just to glisten and leave a trail on top of the soup.

Tip Serve this soup with a side dish of chargrilled Provençal vegetable bruschetta made with day-old French bread. Slice it and bake for about 7–10 minutes in a cool oven – about 140°C (275°F) Gas 1 – drizzled with olive oil and sprinkled with sea salt. On an open fire (if you have one), barbecue or chargrill, cook fine slices of aubergine/eggplant, peppers, red onion and courgette/zucchini. Layer these on the baked bruschetta and stack with sun blushed tomatoes, black olives and fresh basil. These make a wonderful accompaniment to this delicious sunny soup.

GREEN TOMATO & SORREL SOUP

Tangy green tomatoes and lemon-flavoured sorrel combine to make a deliciously refreshing and sophisticated-tasting cold soup. If you can't source fresh sorrel, leaf spinach with a squeeze of lemon juice makes a tasty alternative. Serve as an appetizer or light lunch with bread and butter on the side.

50 g/2 cups sorrel leaves

25 g/2 tablespoons butter

1 shallot, finely chopped

500 g/1 lb. green tomatoes, roughly chopped

600 ml/2½ cups Chicken or Vegetable Stock (see pages 8–9)

sea salt and freshly ground black pepper

4 tablespoon plain yogurt, to garnish

SERVES 4

First, prepare the sorrel. Tear the leaves off the tough ribs and shred the leaves finely.

Melt the butter in a heavy-based saucepan set over a medium heat. Add the shallot and fry gently for 2–3 minutes until softened, stirring now and then. Add the tomatoes and shredded sorrel and continue to cook, stirring often, for 2–3 minutes.

Add the stock to the pan, stir to combine and season with salt and pepper. Bring to the boil, reduce the heat, cover and simmer for 25 minutes.

Blend the soup until smooth, then strain through a fine mesh sieve/strainer set over a jug/pitcher. Cool completely, then chill in the fridge for at least 2 hours.

Serve each portion garnished with a swirl of plain yogurt and seasoned with pepper.

FRESH SPINACH SOUP WITH SLOW-ROASTED TOMATOES

30 g/2 tablespoons butter

1 onion, diced

2 small potatoes, peeled
and diced

800 ml/3⅓ cups Vegetable
Stock (see page 8)

300 g/2 generous cups
fresh or frozen peas

400 g/14 oz. spinach leaves,
any large stalks removed
and roughly chopped if
large leaves

8–10 fresh mint leaves

2 tablespoons freshly chopped
coriander/cilantro

150 ml/⅔ cup double/heavy
cream and sour cream
combined (for a little more
'edge' use all sour cream,
or for a richer soup use all
double/heavy cream)

sea salt and ground
black pepper

slow-roasted cherry tomatoes,
to garnish (optional)

SERVES 4–6

This is a wow of a soup – as green as the summer fields and as fresh as a handful of herbs! If you want to keep it low in fat, a plain yogurt works just as well as cream, and is perfect if you want to serve this soup chilled for a summer lunch.

Melt the butter in a large saucepan set over gentle heat and add the onion and potatoes. Cook for a few minutes, until the butter has been absorbed and the onion has softened, then pour in the stock and simmer for about 15 minutes, until the potatoes are tender. Add the peas and simmer for a further couple of minutes, until they are just soft, being very careful not to overcook them – it is crucial to keep the peas as green as you can. When the peas are tender, add the fresh spinach and immediately draw the pan off the heat. Blend the soup with a stick blender until almost smooth, then add the fresh herbs and continue to blend until silky smooth. Stir in the double/heavy and sour cream and season to taste with salt and pepper.

Ladle the soup into bowls and scatter with a few slow-cooked oven-dried cherry tomatoes, if using, for a wonderful sweet and dramatic finish.

CREAMY LEEK & POTATO SOUP WITH HAM HOCK

This delicious, creamy soup is wonderfully comforting. If you have any leftover ham hock, tear it into bite-size pieces and add to the soup before seasoning and simmer a little while to infuse the flavours. Alternatively, just scatter some good chopped ham on top as a garnish.

50 g/3½ tablespoons butter

4 leeks, whites only, sliced

4 potatoes, peeled and diced

800 m/3⅓ cups Chicken or Vegetable Stock (see pages 8–9)

400 ml/1⅔ cups whole milk

a good slug of double/ heavy cream

cooked ham, shredded (optional)

sea salt and ground black pepper

TO GARNISH

a small handful of fresh parsley, chopped

a small handful of fresh chives, chopped

SERVES 6–8

Melt the butter in a large saucepan and add the leeks and potatoes. Cook for a few minutes, until the butter has been absorbed and the vegetables have softened. Pour in the stock and milk and simmer for 15–20 minutes, until the potatoes and leeks are tender. Draw the pan off the heat and use a stick blender to blend the soup until it is silky smooth. Stir in the cream and add the ham. Season well with salt and pepper.

To serve, ladle the soup into chunky bowls and garnish with a sprinkling of fresh herbs.

PEAR, CELERY & BLUE CHEESE SOUP
WITH SALTED SUGARED WALNUTS

60 g/4 tablespoons salted butter

6 shallots, diced

1 leek, white only, sliced

1 large potato, peeled and diced

½ celeriac/celery root, peeled and diced

1.5 litres/6 cups Vegetable Stock (see page 8)

6 celery sticks, sliced

2 large pears (hard ones are best for this as they are less grainy), peeled, cored and roughly diced

400 g/14 oz. blue cheese (Stilton, dolcelatte or similar), crumbled

a small bunch of fresh flat leaf parsley, chopped

2 tablespoons double/ heavy cream

ground black pepper

baby rocket/arugula leaves, to serve

FOR THE SALTED WALNUTS

½ teaspoon rock salt

1 teaspoon (caster) sugar

a handful of shelled walnuts

a baking sheet, lined with baking paper

SERVES 6–8

Minus the walnuts and rocket/arugula, this soup could be considered to be rather 'old school', but they bring it up to speed! This is delicious, and great after Christmas to use up that old Stilton, especially accompanied by a shot of sloe gin.

Melt the butter in a large saucepan and add the shallots, leek, potato and celeriac/celery root. Sauté until just softened and the butter is absorbed, then cover with the stock and add the celery. Simmer for about 15–20 minutes, until all the vegetables are tender, then toss in the pears and most of the blue cheese, reserving a little to garnish. Simmer for a further 3 minutes or so, until the pears are softened, then draw the pan off the heat and blend well with stick blender until smooth. Stir in the chopped parsley, season with black pepper and stir in the cream to enrich the soup.

To make the salted walnut garnish, preheat the oven to 180°C (350°F) Gas 4.

Combine the rock salt and sugar in a pestle and mortar and pound until the salt is ground down to a powder. Put the walnuts in a plastic bag with the salt and sugar powder and shake it to coat them. Sprinkle the coated nuts onto the prepared baking sheet and toast in the preheated oven for 10–15 minutes until slightly darkened, but do not burn! Leave to cool and as they do they will crisp up.

Serve the soup in rustic bowls, garnished with the salted walnuts, the remaining blue cheese and rocket/arugula leaves.

FENNEL & COURGETTE SOUP
WITH PARMESAN & CRÈME FRAÎCHE

Fresh, locally grown seasonal ingredients give the best flavour, and this is especially true in this soup if you can source fennel and courgette/zucchini locally. The rocket/arugula gives a lovely peppery hit and the crème fraîche, although rich, lifts the flavour to a slightly fresher note.

75 g/5 tablespoons butter

1 large onion, diced

2 potatoes, peeled and diced

2 small fennel bulbs, finely sliced

2 garlic cloves, crushed

1.75 litres/7⅓ cups Vegetable Stock (see page 8)

2 courgettes/zucchini, diced

a large handful of rocket/arugula leaves

100 ml/7 tablespoons double/heavy cream

200 ml/¾ cup crème fraîche

2 tablespoons freshly grated Parmesan cheese, plus extra to garnish

sea salt and ground black pepper

a small bunch of fresh parsley, roughly chopped, to garnish

SERVES 6

Melt the butter in a large saucepan and add the onion, potatoes, fennel and garlic. Cook for a few minutes over medium heat to soften, then pour over the stock. Bring the liquid to a simmer and cook for about 15 minutes, until the fennel is tender. Add the courgettes/zucchini and the rocket/arugula leaves and cook for a further 4 minutes. Draw the pan off the heat and blend with a stick blender until very smooth. Stir in the cream and crème fraîche and the grated Parmesan, and season well with salt and black pepper.

Ladle the soup into bowls and serve garnished with lots of freshly chopped parsley and a sprinkling of Parmesan on top.

BEETROOT & PARSNIP SOUP WITH HORSERADISH

A vibrant soup such as this first draws you in with colour, enticing you to smell, touch and ultimately consume with pleasure... This soup suberbly showcases the myriad good properties of beetroot/beet – the versatile crimson queen of vegetables.

30 g/2 tablespoons butter

1 small onion, diced

1 small potato, peeled and diced

2 parsnips, peeled and diced

800 ml/3⅓ cups Vegetable Stock (see page 8)

2 large (or 4 small) beetroot/ beets, peeled and diced

100 ml/7 tablespoons double/ heavy cream and sour cream combined (for a little more 'edge' use all sour cream, or for a richer soup use all double/heavy cream)

1–2 tablespoons horseradish sauce (preferably homemade and the stronger the better)

a pinch of ground ginger, or to taste

sea salt and ground black pepper

SERVES 6

Melt the butter in a large saucepan set over gentle heat. Add the onion and cook until beginning to soften, then add the potato and parsnips. Pour in the stock and bring to the boil before adding the beetroot/beets. Cover the pan and simmer for about 15 minutes, until all the roots are soft. (Beetroot/beet is very temperature sensitive, so try to make the remainder of the cooking time as quick as possible or the colour will turn brick red rather than the wonderful pink we are aiming for.)

When the vegetables are tender, draw the pan off the heat and blend with a stick blender until a nice nubbly texture is achieved. The parsnips and potato will purée completely, but the beetroot/beet always remains a little grainy – this only adds to the overall texture of the soup, so do not be alarmed!

Stir in the cream and sour cream along with the horseradish and ginger and season with salt and black pepper. Adjust the seasonings to your taste – if you like the heat of ginger or the hit of horseradish, add more! Ladle into bowls and serve.

Tip For a delicious, punchy garnish, you can add Japanese wasabi horseradish to some crème fraîche and swirl on top of the soup, then scatter with chives and a few warm cooked edamame beans for a stunning and fun finish (as shown, left).

WATERCRESS & ASPARAGUS SOUP
WITH BABY BROAD BEANS

Watercress is strong and peppery and full of iron. Add other gems from the kitchen garden, such as asparagus and baby broad/fava beans, to make a delicious, elegant and very pretty soup that is fit for the grandest of tables and most special of occasions.

2 bunches of tender asparagus spears

150 g/1¼ cups baby broad/ fava beans

100 g/7 tablespoons butter

1½ large onions, chopped

4 potatoes, peeled and diced

1.5 litres/6 cups stock

2 bunches of watercress

a pinch of bicarbonate of soda/ baking soda

125 ml/½ cup double/heavy cream, plus extra to serve

sea salt and ground black pepper

SERVES 6–8

Chop the 'pretty' tip off the asparagus spears and set aside to use as a garnish later. Remove the woody ends from the asparagus by gently bending each stalk – where it naturally breaks is where it becomes tender. Discard the woody ends and chop the tender part of the stems into short lengths.

Remove the broad/fava beans from their tough skins.

Melt the butter in a large saucepan and add the onions and potatoes. Cook until just softening, then cover with the stock. Bring to a simmer and cook for about 15 minutes, until the onions and potatoes are soft. Add the asparagus spears and half of the skinned broad/fava beans and cook until almost tender.

Add the watercress to the pan and almost immediately transfer the soup to a blender (a stick blender doesn't work well, as the watercress clings to the blade) and blend until very smooth. Pour the soup back into the pan, add a pinch of bicarbonate of soda/baking soda (which will help the soup retain its vivid green colour), stir in the cream and season with salt and black pepper.

In a separate saucepan, lightly blanch the reserved asparagus tips and broad/fava beans in boiling water for about 3 minutes – they should still be a vivid green – then drain and pat dry.

To serve, ladle the soup into bowls, swirl through a little cream and garnish with the blanched asparagus tips and beans.

CARROT & BUTTERNUT SOUP WITH ORANGE & GINGER

55 g/4 tablespoons butter

2 onions, diced

1 large butternut squash
(or pumpkin), peeled,
deseeded and diced

3 large carrots, peeled and
sliced

1 leek, white only, sliced

a good pinch of cumin seeds

a good pinch of garam masala

a good pinch of ground
turmeric

a pinch of saffron fronds
(optional)

a good pinch of ground ginger
or a 1-cm/½-inch piece of
fresh ginger, peeled and
grated

freshly grated zest and freshly
squeezed juice of 1 large
orange

1.5 litres/6 cups Vegetable
Stock (see page 8)

350 ml/1⅓ cups sour cream

sea salt and ground
black pepper

TO GARNISH
toasted pumpkin seeds

sprigs of fresh thyme or dill

SERVES 6

Halloween is the perfect time to serve this soup. The warming spice and silky smooth texture of the butternut squash is a wonderful golden nectar. Add more spice as you feel the occasion deserves, but perhaps a little less if you are serving to children. Whatever the occasion, this soup is a winner.

Melt the butter in a large saucepan and add the onions, squash, carrots and leek. Toss the vegetables in the butter and cook over medium heat for a few minutes, then stir in the spices and orange zest so that the vegetables are evenly coated. Pour over the stock, cover the pan and simmer for about 15–20 minutes, until the vegetables are tender.

Draw the pan off the heat and blend with a stick blender until very smooth. Stir in the orange juice and sour cream and season to taste with salt and black pepper.

Ladle the soup into bowls and sprinkle with toasted pumpkin seeds and fresh thyme leaves to garnish before serving.

Tip For a really authentic Halloween look, hollow out a large pumpkin (using the pumkin flesh in the soup in place of the butternut squash), and serve the soup from the pumpkin shell.

FIELD MUSHROOM SOUP
WITH PARMESAN, THYME & PANCETTA

When field mushrooms – flat, black-bottomed and some as big as a small plate – pop up, it is the ideal time to conjure up this delicious soup. Remember that mushrooms are fussy creatures and do not like like to be rushed. They are greedy for butter, too, taking it all in while they think about cooking before spitting it out again when they have relented and softened. Add more butter if yours prove too greedy.

100 g/7 tablespoons butter

1 onion, diced

1 garlic clove, crushed

6 small waxy potatoes, peeled and diced

8 large flat field mushrooms, sliced

800 ml/3⅓ cups Vegetable Stock (see page 8)

a muslin/cheesecloth bag filled with bay leaves, a few juniper berries, sprigs of fresh thyme and a few black peppercorns, tied with string

150 ml/⅔ cup double/ heavy cream, plus a little extra to serve

a dollop of Dijon mustard, to taste

150 g/5½ oz. dry-cured bacon, cooked until crispy and cut into long pieces

50 g/½ cup freshly grated Parmesan cheese

fresh thyme leaves, to garnish

SERVES 6

Melt the butter in a large saucepan, add the onion, garlic and potatoes and cook until the onion is softened, but do not allow to brown. Add the field mushrooms and toss around until they start to wilt, adding a little more butter if necessary. When the mushrooms have eventually settled down and reduced in size, pour over the stock. Add your little muslin/cheescloth bag of infusion, cover the pan and turn the heat down to a very low simmer. Somehow the longer this cooks the better it is; !

When the flavours have married – this should take about 40 minutes – draw the pan off the heat and remove the muslin/cheesecloth bag. Stir in the cream and mustard, then blend with a stick blender until smooth.

Serve the soup in big rustic bowls and add a swirl of cream to contrast against the dark grey of the mushrooms. Garnish with the bacon pieces, a sprinkling of Parmesan and a few fresh thyme leaves. Extra bacon and cheese would, of course, also be quite acceptable!

CAULIFLOWER SOUP WITH COCONUT MILK

Spoiler alert! One trick to making soups taste creamy without cream is to use a generous amount of the featured vegetable and use a good-quality food processor to purée it to the right consistency. Another trick is to use a little coconut milk, which can fool any dairy lover. The roasted pumpkin seeds are great for snacking on before they even make it into the soup as a garnish!

30 g/¼ cup pumpkin seeds

2 teaspoons Himalayan salt

1 medium onion, chopped

1 tablespoon olive oil

3 garlic cloves, chopped

1 large head cauliflower
(cut into small florets)

1 tablespoon butter

480 ml/2 cups water

700 ml/3 cups Vegetable Stock
(see page 8)

120 ml/½ cup unsweetened
light coconut milk

SERVES 4–6

Prepare the roasted pumpkin seeds in advance. Preheat the oven to 150°C (300°F) Gas 2. Spread the seeds evenly on an oiled baking sheet and sprinkle half of the salt on top. Roast for about 30 minutes, checking on them after 15 minutes to make sure they are toasting evenly.

In a large saucepan, fry the onion in olive oil over medium–high heat for about 5 minutes or until translucent. Lower the heat slightly, add the garlic, and fry for another minute or so. Remove from the heat.

In a separate frying pan/skillet, fry half of the cauliflower in the butter. Cook until the cauliflower is toasted. Transfer the cooked cauliflower into a bowl and set aside. Repeat the cooking process with the rest of the cauliflower – this prevents overcrowding in the pan to make sure all the ingredients are cooked evenly.

Once your cauliflower is cooked add it all to the pan of fried onion and garlic with the water, remaining salt and vegetable stock. Bring to the boil, then cover and simmer for 30 minutes. Remove from the heat and stir in the coconut milk.

Purée the soup in a food processor. Return to the heat and warm through. To serve, ladle the soup into bowls and garnish with the pumpkin seeds.

TOMATO, RED PEPPER & SWEET POTATO SOUP
WITH BASIL OIL & VEGETABLE CRISPS

The sweet smoked paprika and the gentle heat from the chilli/chile in this comforting soup warm up even the most wind-swept and bitterly cold winter days. The root vegetable crisps/chips work very well with it, adding a lovely and satisfying crunch. Try and get the Spanish brands of sweet smoked paprika that come in little tins, as they have excellent flavour.

300 g/10 oz. baby plum tomatoes – as ripe and red as you can find extra virgin olive oil

sea salt and freshly ground black pepper

2 red onions, chopped

2 red chillies/chiles, seeded and finely chopped

3 garlic cloves, finely chopped

4 red (bell) peppers, seeded and chopped

1 sweet potato, peeled and chopped into cubes

700 ml/3 cups Vegetable Stock (see page 8)

2 teaspoons sweet smoked paprika

8–10 fresh basil leaves

vegetable crisps/chips (you can get these in good supermarkets and any root vegetable will do, eg. parsnip, sweet potato or beet[root])

SERVES 6–8

Preheat the oven to 180°C (350°F) Gas 4.

Toss the tomatoes in a little oil and salt on a baking sheet. Roast in the preheated oven for about 15 minutes, or until they have shrivelled up a bit and the skins have popped open.

Heat 3 tablespoons oil in a heavy-based saucepan over low heat, add the onions, chillies and garlic and sweat out until the onions are translucent. Add 2 pinches of salt. Add the (bell) peppers and potato and cook over low–medium heat for a further 20 minutes or until the vegetables have softened.

Add the roasted tomatoes and all the juices and the vegetable stock. Bring to the boil and simmer for 10 minutes or until all the vegetables are completely soft. Using a food processor or blender, liquidize the soup until smooth. Return to the pan and add the paprika. Season to taste – it will need more salt and some pepper.

Finely chop the basil and mix together with tablespoons olive oil. Ladle the soup into bowls, then with a teaspoon swirl some of the basil oil over the top and lightly place a few vegetable crisps/chips in the middle of the soup. Serve immediately.

LIGHT SOUPS

SPRING VEGETABLE & CHICKEN BROTH
WITH KAFFIR LIME & GREEN HERBS

1 tablespoon very light
   vegetable oil

4 chicken breasts, sliced
   into thin strips

8 spring onions/scallions,
   finely sliced and whites
   and greens separated

3 garlic cloves, crushed

2 green chillies, finely diced

2 lemongrass stalks, bashed
   to release their flavour

800 ml/3⅓ cups Vegetable
   Stock (see page 8)

6 fresh kaffir lime leaves

1 small leek, white only,
   finely sliced

8 celery sticks, finely sliced

2 fennel bulbs, finely sliced

1 courgette/zucchini,
   finely sliced

200 g/1½ cups fresh or
   frozen peas

200 g/1⅓ cups skinned baby
   broad/fava or edamame
   beans

grated zest and freshly
   squeezed juice
   of 1½ limes, or to taste

a handful of fresh parsley,
   roughly chopped

a small handful of fresh
   coriander/cilantro,
   roughly chopped

a small handful of fresh mint,
   roughly chopped

sea salt

SERVES 6

Oh my goodness, how can something this good for you taste so incredible? This heavenly creation is almost fat free, fresh as a summer garden and as aromatic as having your nose in a lime tree! If you like a little Asian influence, this one is for you!

Pour the oil into a large saucepan, pop in the chicken breast while the oil is still cold and stir to coat well. There is very little oil, so a fine coating on the chicken before the heat takes hold will prevent it from sticking to the pan, and breaking up (undesirable, as this soup needs to be almost a clear broth with every exquisite element holding its own.)

As the pan begins to take heat, add the spring onion/scallion whites, garlic, green chillies and lemongrass. Toss around the pan for a couple of minutes, until the chicken becomes white around the outside, then pour on the stock. Add the lime leaves, leek, celery and fennel. Cover the pan and cook over gentle heat for about 7–10 minutes, until the fennel becomes tender but not too soft. This soup needs to keep a little crunch.

At this point, remove the lime leaves and lemongrass if you feel their job is done, or leave them in if you want to make these flavours more pronounced.

Add the courgette/zucchini, peas and beans and cook for a further 3–5 minutes, until tender. Add the lime zest and half of the lime juice, taste, then add the rest of the juice if you feel it needs it, then season with a little salt. Once the flavour is pretty much where you want it, stir in the delicate fresh herbs.

Serve immediately in clean contemporary bowls, which emphasize the pure nature of the broth. Scatter with the sliced spring onion/scallion greens, to garnish.

KOMBU NOODLE BROTH WITH TEMPURA VEGETABLES

A Japanese-style breakfast or lunch that will leave you feeling warm, relaxed and satisfied, and ready to continue with whatever you're doing. Serve in big bowls, sip the soup and use chopsticks to eat the noodles and veggies!

FOR THE SOUP

4 dried shiitake mushrooms

12-cm/4¾-in. strip of kombu seaweed

1.3 litres/5 cups water

2 small leeks

2 small carrots

2-cm/¾-in. piece of fresh ginger, crushed

3 garlic cloves

4 tablespoons dark sesame oil

tamari, to taste

2 tablespoons toasted sesame seeds

100 g/3½ oz. dried soba or udon noodles

FOR THE TEMPURA

110 ml/½ cup ice-cold water

70 g /½ cup unbleached plain/all-purpose flour, refrigerated, plus extra for coating

¼ teaspoon ground turmeric

220 ml/1 scant cup sunflower oil, for frying

a selection of vegetables (courgette/zucchini, pumpkin, celeriac/celery root, sweet potato, onion, etc.), peeled and thinly sliced

sea salt

SERVES 3–4

Place the shiitake and kombu in a saucepan and add water. Cover and let boil, then lower to a medium heat and let cook for 10 minutes. Remove the kombu and shiitake (slice the tops and discard stems), and keep the broth.

In a large saucepan, sauté the vegetables, ginger and garlic in the dark sesame oil for a couple of minutes. Add the sliced shiitake and the broth and let boil for 5–10 minutes. Season with plenty of tamari.

Cook the noodles separately until al dente, just before serving. If you cook them in the broth, they will soak up a lot of water and you'll end up with less soup than planned!

For the tempura, first make the batter. In a bowl, quickly mix the ice-cold water and flour with a whisk and add salt to taste and the turmeric. Do not over-mix – some lumps are alright. To make the tempura crispy, it's very important to use cold ingredients, not mix too much and use the batter for frying immediately.

Pat each vegetable slice dry with paper towels and roll into flour before dipping into the tempura so that he batter doesn't slide off. Heat the sunflower oil in a frying pan and when hot, dip a couple of vegetable pieces in the batter and fry until slightly golden. You will need about 4 pieces of veggies per person. If you feel the batter is too thin and doesn't stick properly to the floured vegetables, add a little more flour.

Drain the tempura vegetables on paper towels and serve immediately. Serve the cooked, drained noodles in the kombu broth sprinkled with the sesame seeds, with the tempura veggies on the side.

DASHI BROTH WITH UDON NOODLES & SILKEN TOFU

200 g/7 oz. dried udon
   noodles

1.5 litres/2½ pints Dashi stock
   made from instant dashi
   stock powder

50 ml/scant ¼ cup dark
   soy sauce

3 tablespoons mirin

2 tablespoons sake

500 g/1 lb. mixed mushrooms,
   including shiitake, oyster
   and enoki

150 g/1 cup sugar snap peas,
   trimmed and cut in half
   lengthways

200 g/2 cups cubed silken/
   soft tofu

2 tablespoons dried wakame
   seaweed

seven-spice powder

SERVES 4

This is a light, delicately flavoured mushroom soup. You should be able to buy most of the mushrooms fairly readily from larger supermarkets or online, but could substitute like for like with any mushrooms you are able to find.

Plunge the noodles into a saucepan of boiling water and cook for 4–5 minutes or until al dente. Drain, refresh under cold water and shake dry. Set aside.

Pour the broth, soy sauce, mirin and sake into a saucepan set over a medium heat and bring to the boil. Add the mushrooms except the enoki and simmer gently for 5 minutes until the mushrooms are tender. Stir in the sugar snap peas and enoki mushrooms and simmer for 2 minutes.

Divide the noodles between warmed bowls and top with the tofu and seaweed, pour over the soup and serve at once, sprinkled with seven-spice powder.

CAMBODIAN RICE NOODLE & FISH SOUP

250 g/9 oz. dried rice stick noodles

350 g/11 oz. bream or snapper fillets, cut into 2.5-cm/1-in. pieces

250 ml/1 cup Chicken stock (see page 9)

125 ml/½ cup coconut cream

125 ml/½ cup coconut milk

1 tablespoon fish sauce

2 teaspoons grated palm sugar

LEMON GRASS PASTE

6 lemongrass stalks

2.5 cm/1 in. fresh galangal, peeled and roughly chopped

2.5 cm/1 in. fresh turmeric, peeled and roughly chopped

2 kaffir lime leaves, shredded

2 garlic cloves, roughly chopped

2 tablespoons chopped peanuts

1 teaspoon shrimp paste

1 teaspoon freshly grated ginger

TO SERVE

½ cucumber, sliced

60 g/1 cup beansprouts

lotus root (optional)

SERVES 4

Known as 'num banh chok' or more simply 'khmer noodles', this is a classic Cambodian soup traditionally served at breakfast or as an afternoon snack. Although you will find regional differences it is always made with a freshly pounded lemon grass paste, fish, noodles and a selection of crisp raw vegetables and fresh herbs.

Soak the noodles in a bowlful of hot water for 20 minutes until softened. Drain well using a kitchen cloth and set aside.

To make the lemon grass paste, discard the hard end of the lemongrass stalk and peel away and discard the hard outer leaves until you reach the soft core of the stalk. Trim lengths of about 5 cm/2 in. and roughly chop the remaining core. Place the lemon grass in a food processor with the remaining ingredients and blend to a smooth paste.

Heat the oil in a wok or saucepan set over a medium heat until it starts to shimmer. Add the paste and fry for 2–3 minutes until fragrant. Add the fish pieces and fry gently for 2 minutes until cooked. Remove the fish from the pan as carefully as you can and set aside.

Add the stock, coconut cream and coconut milk to the pan and simmer gently for 10 minutes until thick and creamy. Stir in the fish sauce and sugar, and simmer for a final minute.

Divide the noodles between bowls and top with the pieces of fish. Pour over the broth and serve with bowls of sliced cucumber, beansprouts and lotus root (if using).

MISO SOUP WITH MUSHROOMS & GREEN BEANS

10 g/⅓ oz. instant dashi
  stock powder

900 ml/4 cups boiling water

1 tablespoon red miso paste

1 teaspoon vegetable oil

1-cm/⅜-inch piece of root
  ginger, chopped

1 spring onion/scallion,
  finely chopped

a dash of mirin or dry sherry

50 g/⅓ cup green beans,
  cut into short lengths

150 g/5 oz. assorted fresh
  shiitake, oyster and
  shiro-simeji mushrooms,
  the shiitake sliced
  1-cm/⅜-inch thick

SERVES 4

**A wonderfully quick, Japanese-inspired light lunch or supper –
so perfect when you need a meal in a hurry!**

Mix the dashi stock powder into the boiling water and stir until
dissolved. Mix 3 tablespoons of the hot dashi stock with the miso
paste to thin it out. Set both aside.

Heat the oil in a large saucepan over a medium heat. Fry the
ginger and sliced white part of the spring onion/scallion, stirring,
for 1 minute. Add the dashi stock, a dash of mirin or dry sherry
and the thinned miso paste, stirring it in well. Bring to the boil,
then stir in the green beans and assorted mushrooms.

Simmer for 3–5 minutes; you want the mushrooms and the
green beans to retain their texture. Portion into bowls and serve
at once, garnished with the green part of the chopped spring
onion/scallion.

SUMMER CORN SOUP WITH RED PEPPER TAPENADE

Buying locally grown or sourced foods is a popular message today and the ethos resonates here in this simple recipe – to really savour its delightful sweetness, sweetcorn/corn should be eaten really fresh, so do try and get your hands on cobs still wrapped in their husks that are no more than a day or two from the field.

8 fresh corn-on-the-cobs/
kernels from 8 ears of
sweetcorn/corn
(about 6 cups)

1 onion, chopped

1 celery stick/rib, chopped

2 garlic cloves, chopped

40 g/3 tablespoons butter

1.5 litres/6 cups Vegetable
Stock (see page 8)

125 ml/½ cup single/
light cream

1 small bunch of fresh chives,
snipped

sea salt and freshly ground
black pepper

crusty bread, to serve

RED (BELL) PEPPER TAPENADE

1 large red (bell) pepper

1 garlic clove, chopped

50g/⅓ cup pine nuts,
lightly toasted

2 tablespoons olive oil

50 g/⅓ cup Parmesan
cheese, finely grated

SERVES 4

To make the tapenade, preheat the oven to 220°C (425°F) Gas 7. Put the red (bell) pepper on a preheated baking sheet and roast it in the preheated oven for about 15 minutes, turning often until the skin is starting to blacken and puff up. Transfer to a clean plastic bag and let cool. When cool enough to handle, peel off the skin and discard. Roughly chop the flesh and put it in a food processor. Add the garlic, pine nuts and oil and process until smooth. Spoon into a bowl, add the Parmesan and stir well to combine. Set aside until needed.

Carefully shuck the corn kernels from the cobs and put them in a large saucepan. Add the onion, celery, garlic and butter and season well with salt and pepper. Set over medium heat and partially cover with a lid. Cook for 10 minutes, shaking the pan often. Add the stock, bring to the boil and let boil for 15 minutes. Remove from the heat and let cool for about 20 minutes.

Transfer the mixture to a food processor and whizz until smooth. Force the mixture through a fine sieve/strainer and return it to a clean saucepan. Add the cream and gently reheat, stirring constantly. Ladle the soup into warmed serving bowls, top with a dollop of the Red (Bell) Pepper Tapenade, sprinkle with chives and serve with thick slices of good, crusty bread, if liked.

THAI-STYLE TOMATO GAZPACHO

This Southeast Asian take on a classic Spanish gazpacho is a wonderfully refreshing dish, perfect for summer entertaining. For optimum flavour, choose the ripest, tastiest tomatoes you can find.

700 g/1½ lbs. ripe tomatoes

2 lemon grass stalks

1 garlic clove, peeled

1 red onion, peeled and chopped

a 5-cm/2-in. piece of fresh ginger, peeled and chopped

150 ml/⅔ cup tomato juice

2 tablespoons rice or white wine vinegar

2 tablespoons olive oil

salt and freshly ground black pepper

6 kaffir lime leaves

1 red (bell) pepper, deseeded and finely diced

¼ cucumber, finely diced

SERVES 4

Begin by scalding the tomatoes. Pour boiling water over the ripe tomatoes in a heatproof bowl. Set aside for 1 minute, then drain and carefully peel off the skin using a sharp knife. Set aside.

Peel the tough outer casing from the lemon grass stalks. Finely chop the white, lower, bulbous part of each stalk, discarding the remaining fibrous stalk.

In a food processor, blend the peeled tomatoes, lemon grass, garlic, onion, ginger, tomato juice, vinegar and oil until finely chopped. Transfer the mixture to a large jug/pitcher. Stir in 150 ml/⅔ cup of water and season with salt and pepper.

Tear the kaffir lime leaves into shreds, discarding the central vein, and mix into the gazpacho. Cover and chill in the fridge for at least 4 hours.

To serve, pour the gazpacho into bowls and garnish with diced (bell) pepper and cucumber.

THAI MUSHROOM & LEMONGRASS BROTH

2 lemongrass stalks

200 g/6½ oz. assorted oyster, shimeji and button mushrooms; if unavailable use button mushrooms

1 tablespoon olive oil

1 onion, chopped

2.5-cm/1-inch piece of root ginger, chopped

1 litre/4 cups Chicken Stock (see page 9)

4 kaffir lime leaves

2 fresh red chillies/chiles

2–3 tablespoons fish sauce, or to taste

juice of ½ lime or ½ lemon

a handful of fresh coriander/cilantro, to garnish

salt

SERVES 4

This is a clear, flavourful Thai-style broth, with appealing citrus notes, which showcases the tender texture of fresh mushrooms beautifully.

Trim the lemongrass stalks of their tough outer casing. Finely chop the soft, lower, bulbous white part of each stalk. Slice the oyster mushrooms and button mushrooms.

Heat the oil in a large saucepan over a medium heat. Add the onion, ginger and lemongrass and fry, stirring, for 1–2 minutes until the onion has softened and the mixture is fragrant. Add the stock, lime leaves and whole chillies/chiles. Season to taste with salt.

Bring to the boil. Add the fish sauce and lime juice. Taste to check the seasoning; you want a salty, tangy flavour. Bring the soup to the boil once more. Add the mushrooms, then lower the heat and simmer for 2 minutes until just tender. Ladle into bowls and serve at once garnished with the fresh coriander/cilantro.

LETTUCE & COURGETTE SOUP WITH CHERVIL

12 sweet shallots, diced

1 large potato, peeled and diced

40 g/3 tablespoons butter

1.5 litres/6 cups Chicken
   or Vegetable Stock
   (see pages 8–9)

2 garlic cloves, crushed

4 courgettes/zucchini, diced

1 large, plump flat lettuce
   or large Little Gem/Bibb
   lettuces, finely sliced

200 ml/¾ cup double/
   heavy cream

a good bunch of fresh chervil,
   chopped, plus a few whole
   leaves to garnish

a squeeze of lemon juice

sea salt and ground
   black pepper

SERVES 6–8

The understated nature of this soup makes it special. It mixes simplicity with opulence thereby appealing to all comers from elegant diners to hearty outdoor types. This soup can be eaten hot or cold, so you can adapt it to the unpredictable weather.

In a large heavy-based saucepan, sweat the shallots and potato in the butter for a few minutes, until they are softened. Pour in the stock and add the garlic, then simmer for about 15 minutes, until the potato is tender. Add the courgettes/zucchini to the pan and continue to simmer for a further 2–3 minutes, until the they are just tender but still nice and bright green. Do not overcook, as the colour will fade and the freshness of flavour will be lost.

Add the lettuce to the pan, then draw the pan off the heat. Using a stick blender, purée the soup until nice and smooth. Stir in the cream and chopped chervil, season to taste with salt and black pepper and sharpen the soup with a squeeze of lemon juice.

Ladle the soup into bowls and serve garnished with a few chervil leaves.

FRENCH ONION SOUP WITH COMTÉ CROUTES

The key to a perfect French onion soup is to cook your onions for a seriously long time until they are reduced to an unctuous, sticky, golden mass. Rich beef stock and a cheesy croûte top off this classic.

25 g/2 tablespoons unsalted butter

3 tablespoons olive oil

1 kg/2¼ lb. large onions, very thinly sliced

250 ml/generous 1 cup dry white wine

1 litre/4 cups rich Beef Stock (see page 9)

freshly grated nutmeg

a small handful of fresh thyme sprigs

2 fresh bay leaves

75 ml/⅓ cup good-quality Madeira

1 day-old French or other crusty bread, cut into slices

1 garlic clove, peeled

150 g/5 oz. Comté cheese, grated

sea salt and ground black pepper

SERVES 4

Melt the butter in a heavy-based pan or flameproof casserole and add the oil. Add the onions and season with salt. Cook over a low heat, stirring occasionally, for at least 45 minutes until they have reduced right down to a golden, sticky mass.

Add the wine and bubble, stirring, for a minute, then add the beef stock, a good grating of nutmeg and the herbs. Simmer for 20 minutes, then add the Madeira and bubble for 5 minutes more. Check the seasoning and spoon into four small ovenproof bowls or dishes.

Preheat the grill/broiler to high. Toast the slices of crusty bread and rub one side all over with the garlic. Put the toasts on top of the bowls so that they cover the surface of the soup. Sprinkle with lots and lots of cheese and put on a baking sheet under the grill/broiler until the soup is bubbling and the toasts are oozingly melted and golden. Serve straight away.

SUMMER MINESTRONE WITH CHICKPEAS & PECORINO

Minestrone can be defined as a hotchpotch of whatever takes your fancy. Often thought of as cold-weather fare, this version has summer written all over it and is packed with fresh tomatoes and green beans as well as that pantry staple, chickpeas/garbanzo beans. As if it weren't already summery enough, a few handfuls of rocket/arugula add a peppery bite to lighten the soup.

2 tablespoons olive oil

1 onion, chopped

2 garlic cloves, chopped

400-g/14-oz. can chickpeas/ garbanzo beans, rinsed and drained

100 g/4 oz. green beans, sliced on the angle

6 ripe tomatoes, halved

1 handful of chopped fresh flat leaf parsley

1.5 litres/6 cups Vegetable Stock (see page 8)

100 g/3½ oz. wholemeal/ whole-wheat spaghetti, broken into 3–4-cm/2-inch pieces

2 handfuls of wild rocket/ arugula

50 g/1 cup finely grated Pecorino Romano cheese

sea salt and freshly ground black pepper

crusty bread, to serve

SERVES 4

Put the oil in a large saucepan set over medium heat. Add the onion, partially cover with a lid and cook for 4–5 minutes, stirring often, until softened. Add the garlic and cook for 1 minute. Add the chickpeas, green beans, tomatoes, parsley, stock and spaghetti and bring to the boil.

Reduce the heat and let simmer for 40 minutes, stirring often, until the pasta is cooked and the soup is thick. Season to taste with salt and pepper.

Just before serving, add the rocket/arugula and gently stir until the leaves soften. Ladle into warmed serving bowls and sprinkle a generous amount of grated Pecorino over the top. Serve immediately with chunks of crusty bread.

Next time Try making this delicious soup with different vegetables. Courgettes/zucchini and carrots are a nice addition but remember that both take a little longer to cook so dice them very finely before adding to the soup with the other vegetables. A pinch of smoky Spanish paprika (pimentón) will add a slightly different flavour.

CAJUN-STYLE QUINOA SOUP WITH RED BEANS & KALE

This is a great take on a Southern Cajun soup, using the superfoods kale and quinoa. Taking the step to purée some of the beans and stock is necessary to get the perfect consistency but if you are busy you can substitute kidney beans from a can. Wilting the kale makes it easier to digest.

175 g/1 cup dried red
  kidney beans

1 onion, chopped

1 green (bell) pepper, chopped

2 celery stalks, chopped

2 tablespoons olive oil

2 garlic cloves, finely chopped

300 ml/1¼ cups Vegetable
  Stock (see page 8)

750 ml/3 cups water

160 g/¾ cup quinoa

2 teaspoons dried oregano

a pinch of cayenne pepper

2 teaspoons paprika

100 g/1 large bunch kale

sea salt and freshly ground
  black pepper, to taste

SERVES 4–6

Put the dry red kidney beans in a bowl and soak in water overnight. When you are ready to make the soup, drain and set aside.

In a large saucepan, heat the onion, green (bell) pepper and celery in oil over a medium heat. Cook for about 3 minutes or until the onion is translucent. Then add the garlic, stir and cook for another minute. Put the drained red kidney beans into the pan with the vegetable stock and water. Bring the liquid to the boil then reduce the heat, cover and simmer until the beans are tender. This usually takes around 50 minutes.

Remove 500 ml/2 cups of the stock and 2 teaspoons of the beans and purée in a food processor. Then return the thickened purée to the pan.

Now add the quinoa, herbs and spices. Return to the boil, then reduce the heat, cover and simmer for 15 minutes. Meanwhile, prepare the kale.

Wash the kale in cold water. Then trim the stems and rough chop the leaves. After the quinoa has been cooking for 15 minutes, add the kale. Cover and continue to cook for another 8 minutes, until the quinoa is fully cooked.

Add salt and pepper to taste and serve immediately.

CHINESE CHICKEN SOUP WITH BLACK FORBIDDEN RICE

Black rice has its origin in China and has a pleasantly mild, nutty flavour to go with its striking colour. It is always worth cooking this chicken soup the traditional way: that is, a day ahead to allow time for the flavours to fully develop.

CHICKEN BROTH

1 chicken (cut into 8 pieces, bones and skin left on)

4 carrots

1 onion, peeled and quartered

1 parsnip

2 celery stalks

1 bay leaf

4 sprigs of fresh dill

a handful of chopped fresh flat-leaf parsley

130 g/1 cup cooked black rice (see method)

2 carrots, chopped

1 celery stalk, chopped

a handful of chopped fresh flat-leaf parsley and dill, to garnish

SERVES 4

Put all of the chicken broth ingredients in a large saucepan on a medium–high heat. Cover with water and bring to the boil. Reduce the heat, cover and simmer for 1 hour.

Remove the white breast meat so that it doesn't overcook, cool and set aside in the refrigerator. Return the bones to the pan and simmer for another hour. Strain the broth and chill in the refrigerator overnight. You can eat the overcooked veggie mush, but discard it if you prefer.

The next day, cut or shred the chicken into pieces. Then cook the black rice according to packet instruction or using the ratio of 200 g/1 cup of rice to 420 ml/1¾ cups of water.

Put the rice and water in a medium saucepan and bring to the boil. Reduce to a low heat, cover and simmer for 30 minutes. Remove from the heat, fluff with a fork, then put the lid back on and set aside for 5 minutes.

Skim the fat off the top of the broth and pour into a large saucepan. Add in the carrots, celery and black rice. Cook for about 5 minutes or until the vegetables are tender, then add the shredded chicken and cook until heated through.

Serve immediately and garnish with chopped parsley and dill.

GREEN DETOX SOUP WITH HEMP SEEDS

If chicken soup (see previous recipe) as a cure-all doesn't appeal to you when you are unwell, cooked greens may be the answer. Whatever ails you, this recipe is easy to throw together when you are feeling under the weather and is also an excellent choice to jumpstart a new dietary regime.

1 tablespoon butter

1 tablespoon olive oil

1 medium onion, chopped

2 garlic cloves, chopped

500 g/18 oz (about 4 medium) courgettes/zucchini

240 ml/1 cup water

480 ml/2 cups Vegetable Stock (see page 8)

100 g/3½ oz fresh spinach

1 tablespoon sea salt

1 teaspoon freshly ground black pepper

a handful of chopped mint, plus extra

TO GARNISH

2 tablespoons milled hemp seeds

4 tablespoons crème fraîche, to garnish

SERVES 4–6

Heat the butter and oil in a large saucepan over a high heat.

Fry the onion in the saucepan for 10 minutes or until translucent. Add the garlic then reduce the temperature and add the courgettes/zucchini, water and stock to the pan. Slowly bring to the boil, then cover and simmer for 10 minutes.

At the end, add the spinach, season, and cook for a further 5 minutes.

Set aside to cool slightly.

Once cooled, purée the soup with the mint and hemp seeds in a food processor. Return to the heat and warm through. Serve in bowls and garnish with a dollop of crème fraîche and a few small mint leaves.

HEARTY SOUPS

CHUNKY PROVENÇAL VEGETABLE & BEAN SOUP
WITH SMOKED PAPRIKA

50 ml/3½ tablespoons olive oil

1 red onion, diced

2 garlic cloves, crushed

½ courgette/zucchini, diced

1 carrot, peeled and diced

2 celery sticks, sliced

1 small leek, white only, sliced

800 ml/3⅓ cups Vegetable Stock (see page 8)

a 400-g/14-oz. can chopped tomatoes

50 g/3½ tablespoons tomato purée/paste

a good pinch of smoked paprika

200 g/7 oz. mixed canned butter/lima beans and kidney beans, drained

a small handful of green beans, sliced into short lengths

1 tablespoon balsamic vinegar

a small bunch of fresh basil, roughly chopped

a small bunch of fresh parsley, roughly chopped

sea salt and ground black pepper

SERVES 6–8

This is such a simple and quick soup, and you can use up little left-over bits of vegetable, as only small amounts of each are needed. The quantities and ingredients below are a rough guide because really you can use whatever you happen to have in your fridge. The smoked paprika and balsamic bring it together to give a great balance of interest on the palate.

Put the olive oil, onion, garlic, courgette/zucchini, carrot, celery and leek in a large saucepan and toss over medium heat for about 3–4 minutes, until they have taken up the oil.

Pour in the stock and chopped tomatoes, then add the green beans and tomato purée/paste and stir everything together. Simmer for about 15–20 minutes, until the vegetables are tender.

Add the smoked paprika, mixed beans and balsamic vinegar to the pan, cooking for a minute to heat the beans through. Season to taste with salt and black pepper and stir everything together. Finally, stir in the freshly chopped basil and parsley, reserving a little to garnish.

Ladle the soup into chunky rustic bowls and serve scattered with the reserved fresh herbs.

VELVETY PUMPKIN & RED LENTIL SOUP
WITH TURMERIC

This is a favourite soup for when the weather turns and winter approaches. It is so rich and delicious, you'll find it hard to resist licking your plate, spoon and even the saucepan!

70 g/½ cup chopped leek (white part) or onion

4 tablespoons olive oil

a pinch of sea salt

200 g/1⅔ cups peeled and seeded pumpkin or squash wedges cut into 3–4-cm/1¼–1½-in. pieces

120 g/1 cup carrot cut into 2–3 cm/¼-1¼ in. pieces

1 teaspoon vegetable bouillon powder

¼ teaspoon ground turmeric

4 garlic cloves, crushed

2 bay leaves

3 dried tomato halves, chopped

2 tablespoons cooking wine

150 g/¾ cup dried red lentils, washed and drained

7-cm/2¾-in. strip of kombu seaweed

1 litre/4 cups water

a squeeze of lemon juice

a little crushed black pepper

1 tablespoon umeboshi vinegar

SERVES 4

In a large saucepan, sauté the leek or onions in the olive oil with the salt, uncovered, until they're soft and transparent.

Add the pumpkin or squash and carrot and sauté until the veggies start to 'sweat'. Add the bouillon powder, turmeric, garlic, bay leaves and tomatoes and stir. Next, pour in the wine and let the mixture boil. Now it's time to add the lentils, kombu and water. Turn up the heat, cover and bring to the boil. Then, lower the heat and let simmer for about 25–30 minutes or until the lentils and vegetables are completely tender.

At this point, remove the bay leaves and leave the soup as it is, if you like it chunky and stew-like or use a stick blender to purée the soup and make it creamy. Add the lemon juice, crushed pepper, and umeboshi vinegar and stir. Taste and add more spices if desired. The soup will thicken as it cools so you can add more hot water if it seems too thick.

Tip Adding 80 g/⅔ cup diced beetroot/beet cubes together with the pumpkin and carrot will give this soup a nice earthy aroma and a lovely reddish-orange hue.

RATATOUILLE SOUP
WITH GOATS' CHEESE, BLACK OLIVES & BASIL

The markets in the Mediterranean are an inspiration, and you can make this wonderful rustic soup by throwing together a bit of everything you might find on the vegetable stall... no fuss, no bother and whatever the weather! This soup is wonderful with a round of fresh young goats' cheese served on top – just allow it to sit there for a moment before serving and see it melt around the outside.

1 large aubergine/eggplant, chopped into 1-cm/½-inch thick slices, then in half again into half moons

1 large red onion, chopped into quarters, then quarters again

½ fennel bulb, cut into slim wedges

4 garlic cloves, whole and skin on

200 ml/¾ cup olive oil

2 courgettes/zucchini, roughly diced (but keep chunky)

2 red (bell) peppers

2 yellow (bell) peppers

6 ripe tomatoes, roughly chopped

600 ml/2½ cups passata (Italian sieved tomatoes)

500 ml/2 cups tomato juice or Vegetable Stock (see page 8)

a small handful of stoned/pitted black olives

a small bunch of fresh basil, chopped

sea salt and ground black pepper

sliced goats' cheese, to serve

SERVES 6

Preheat the oven to 200°C (400°F) Gas 6.

Put the aubergine/eggplant, red onion and fennel into a heavy roasting pan with the garlic cloves and drizzle with most of the olive oil. Roast in the preheated oven for about 15 minutes, until soft and slightly blackened, turning the vegetables once during cooking for an even colour. Towards the end of the cooking time, add the diced courgettes/zucchini to the pan and mix in with the other vegetables so that they cook for a few minutes and pick up a little colour and flavour.

Cut the (bell) peppers in half and remove the seeds. Lay them skin-side up in a separate roasting pan and brush them with the remaining olive oil. Roast until the skin is beginning to blister – about 15 minutes (these can cook at the same time as the other vegetables). Leave to cool, then remove the skins and cut the peppers into strips.

Put all the roast vegetables (including any oil from the roasting pans) into a large saucepan. Squeeze the flesh out of the garlic cloves and add to the pan, discarding the skins. Add the chopped tomatoes and passata and cook over gentle heat, stirring, for about 20 minutes, until the passata has reduced and the vegetables have softened and are merging together. Add the tomato juice until a soupy but quite thick consistency is achieved (you may not need it all), then season with sea salt and black pepper. Finally, stir in the black olives and basil.

Ladle the soup into bowls and serve each topped with a slice of goats' cheese.

SWEET POTATO & COCONUT SOUP WITH THAI PESTO

1 tablespoon light olive oil

500 g/1 lb. sweet potato, peeled and chopped into chunks

1 red onion, chopped

1 tablespoon Thai red curry paste

500 ml/2 cups Vegetable Stock (see page 8)

500 ml/2 cups coconut milk

THAI PESTO

100 g/⅔ cup unsalted peanuts, lightly toasted

2 garlic cloves, chopped

2 teaspoons finely grated fresh ginger

2 large green chillies/chiles, deseeded and chopped

1 small bunch of fresh coriander/cilantro

1 large handful of fresh mint leaves

1 large handful of fresh basil leaves

2 tablespoons light soy sauce or Thai fish sauce

2 tablespoons freshly squeezed lime juice

1 tablespoon soft light brown sugar

SERVES 4

Sweet potatoes make an excellent ingredient for soups since when blended they take on a velvety, creamy texture. Here, their sweetness is cut through with some full-on spicy Asian flavours in the form of a Thai-style pesto, which really brings this soup to life.

Put the oil in a heavy-based saucepan set over medium heat. Add the sweet potato and onion, partially cover with a lid and cook for 15 minutes, stirring often, until they are soft and just starting to turn golden. Increase the heat to high, add the curry paste and stir-fry with the sweet potato for 3–4 minutes so that the paste cooks and becomes fragrant. Add the stock and coconut milk and bring to the boil. Transfer the mixture to a food processor or blender and whizz until smooth. Return the soup to a clean saucepan.

To make the pesto, put all of the ingredients in a food processor or blender and whizz, occasionally scraping down the sides of the bowl, until you have a chunky green paste and the ingredients are all evenly chopped. Gently reheat the soup, then ladle into warmed serving bowls. Top with a generous spoonful of Thai pesto to serve.

ROOT VEGETABLE & GROUND BEEF SOUP

2–3 tablespoons vegetable oil

250 g/9 oz. minced/
ground beef

1 small onion, diced

2 large garlic cloves, crushed

½ swede/rutabaga, peeled
and diced

1 small carrot, peeled and diced

½ celeriac/celery root, peeled
and diced

2 celery sticks, sliced

1 small leek, white only, sliced

1 small potato, peeled and
diced

a 400-g/14-oz. can chopped
tomatoes

800 ml/3⅓ cups Beef Stock
(see page 9)

60 g/4 generous tablespoons
tomato purée/paste

250 g/1¾ cups frozen
or fresh peas

a small bunch of fresh parsley,
chopped, plus extra to
garnish

a few sprigs of fresh thyme

a splash of Worcestershire
sauce (optional)

sea salt and ground
black pepper

SERVES 6

This is a mainstay warming lunch when the weather outside is cold and your time is short. It can be cooked ahead of time and left in the fridge for up to four days, and will only get better. You can use lamb instead of beef and add a little rosemary. Equally, if you have some meat left from the Sunday joint, you can mince/grind or roughly chop it up and use that instead. As for the vegatables, just make up to the correct volume with your own choices to use up leftovers!

Melt the oil in a large heavy-based saucepan. Toss in the beef and fry until browned, stirring all the time to brown the meat. Add the onion and garlic and continue to cook until the onion is translucent and softened.

Add all the vegetables and stir them into the meat and onions, making sure there is no clumping of any one ingredient – you want them evenly dispersed. Add the chopped tomatoes, beef stock and tomato purée/paste and put the lid on the pan. Allow to simmer gently for about 12 minutes, or until the vegetables are almost soft – you don't want them mushy, as a little 'al dente' adds to the eating experience. Now add the peas and herbs and season with salt and black pepper. If you want a little extra flavour, add a splash of Worcestershire sauce and simmer for a few more minutes to let all the flavours marry, before spooning into warmed bowls, to serve.

Tip If you are not eating the soup immediately, the peas are better added just before the soup is required, so that they retain their lovely green colour. This soup is perfect served with delicious multi-grain bread and unsalted butter, but to make it into even more of a meal, you could also add lovely herby dumplings: serve one or two with each portion and scatter with plenty of fresh parsley.

EASY MINESTRONE WITH SPAGHETTI

Everyone should have a basic minestrone recipe in their repertoire. It is the most comforting and nourishing of soups – the perfect balanced meal-in-a-bowl. This is a great one to start with and then put your own spin on according to the season, and what you have in your fridge that needs using up!

2 tablespoons olive oil

4 rashers/slices of bacon, chopped

1 large onion, diced

3 carrots, peeled and diced

1 celery stick, sliced

1 leek, sliced

3 potatoes, peeled and diced

2 garlic cloves, crushed

a 400-g/14-oz. can chopped tomatoes

1.5 litres/6 cups Vegetable Stock (see page 8)

a handful (about 70 g/2½ oz.) of broken spaghetti, or similar

a 400-g/14-oz. can cannellini or haricot/navy beans, drained

250 g/9 oz. spinach or other greens, chopped

1–2 courgettes/zucchini, diced

a bunch of fresh parsley, chopped

1 teaspoon mixed dried herbs

paprika, to taste (optional)

sea salt and ground black pepper

freshly grated Parmesan cheese, to serve

SERVES 6

Heat the olive oil in a large saucepan and fry the bacon until browned. Add the onion, carrots, celery, leek and potatoes, put the lid on the pan and sweat for a few minutes over gentle heat, until the vegetables soften without colouring. Add the garlic to the pan and continue cooking for a few minutes before adding the chopped tomatoes, stock and pasta. Bring the liquid to the boil, then reduce to a simmer and cook until the vegetables are just tender and the pasta is almost cooked. Add the beans, greens, courgettes/zucchini and parsley to the pan and continue to cook for a few minutes until the greens are tender but still green. Season to taste with salt and pepper and, if you like a little heat, stir in a little paprika.

Serve generous portions of the soup in big flat bowls and finish with lots of freshly grated Parmesan.

PUY LENTIL & BACON SOUP WITH SEASONAL GREENS

2–3 tablespoons olive oil

150 g/4 oz. bacon lardons or thick-cut dry cured bacon cut into matchsticks

1 small onion, chopped

4 garlic cloves, crushed

1 leek, sliced

1 celery stick, sliced

2 carrots, peeled and sliced

¼ celeriac/celery root, peeled and diced

¼ swede/rutabaga, peeled and diced

125 g/⅔ cup Puy lentils, rinsed and drained

1.3 litres/5½ cups Vegetable Stock (see page 8)

a 400-g/14-oz. can chopped tomatoes

1½ tablespoons tomato purée/paste

¼ small savoy cabbage or other greens (cut as a chiffonade, long and very fine)

a small handful of fresh parsley, chopped

a small handful of fresh thyme, chopped

sea salt and ground black pepper

SERVES 6–8

A particularly beautiful savoy cabbage was the inspiration for this soup, but you can make it your own with your favourite green leafy vegetables when they are in season – try sweetheart cabbage and spring greens when available. Use a nice big heavy-based pan to slowly cook and hold the heat evenly through the soup, and cut all your vegetables to about the same size so they cook evenly.

Put the olive oil in a large heavy-based saucepan, add the bacon, onion and garlic and cook until the onion is softened and the bacon is just cooked. Add the leek, celery, carrots, celeriac/celery root and swede/rutabaga to the pan, along with the Puy lentils. Stir to coat all the vegetables with the oil so that they absorb a little and glisten slightly, then pour over the stock and chopped tomatoes and season with salt and pepper. Put the lid on the pan and simmer very gently for about 15 minutes – you do not want a ferocious boil or the bacon will break up, and it is nice to have each element of this soup holding its own.

Draw the pan off the heat and stir in the tomato purée/paste, greens and chopped fresh herbs. Return to the heat and simmer until the greens are just tender but retain a little crunch.

Ladle the soup into rustic bowls, to serve.

GENTLY SPICED CHICKEN & VEGETABLE SOUP
WITH COCONUT & GINGER

2 tablespoons light
  vegetable oil

1 garlic clove, crushed

a 3-cm/1¼-inch piece of
  fresh ginger, grated

1 red chilli/chile, finely chopped

6–7 spring onions/scallions,
  finely sliced and whites
  and greens separated

1 red (bell) pepper, deseeded
  and finely sliced

1 green (bell) pepper, deseeded
  and finely sliced

4 carrots, peeled and very
  finely sliced

2 celery sticks, very finely
  sliced

300 ml/1¼ cups coconut milk

750 ml/3 cups Vegetable Stock
  (see page 8)

1 tablespoon tomato
  purée/paste

500 g/1 lb. cooked chicken

a squeeze of lime juice

a splash of fish sauce

a handful of fresh coriander/
  cilantro, chopped

a small handful of sugar snap
  peas, sliced lengthways

sea salt and ground
  black pepper

chilli oil and lime wedges,
  to serve (optional)

SERVES 6

Close your eyes when you taste this lovely broth and the fresh lime and coconut flavours will transport you to a beach café in Thailand. It is deliciously elegant with plenty of attitude to make it interesting.

Put the oil in a large saucepan set over high heat. Throw in the garlic, ginger, chilli/chile and spring onion/scallion whites. Toss around the pan for a few seconds, then add the red and green (bell) peppers, carrots and celery to the pan, followed by the coconut milk and stock. Stir in the tomato purée/paste and add the cooked chicken, then pop the lid on the pan and simmer for a few minutes, until the vegetables are wilted and the chicken is heated through. Season to taste, adding a squeeze of lime juice, a splash of fish sauce and the chopped coriander/cilantro.

Just before you are ready to serve, throw in the sugar snap peas and the sliced spring onion/scallion greens. Ladle the soup into bowls and serve drizzled with a little chilli oil, and with lime wedges on the side, if wished.

250 g/9 oz. dried rice stick
  noodles

2 large skinless chicken breast
  fillets (about 350 g/12 oz.)

1 litre/4 cups Chicken Stock
  (see page 9)

2 tablespoons vegetable oil

400 ml/1²/₃ cups coconut milk

200 ml/³/₄ cup coconut cream

2 tablespoons fish sauce

2 teaspoons caster/
  granulated sugar

LAKSA PASTE

6 shallots, chopped

4 garlic cloves, chopped

2 lemon grass stalks,
  thinly sliced

2 large red bird's eye chillies/
  chiles, deseeded and sliced

2.5 cm/1 in. fresh galangal,
  peeled and chopped

2.5 cm/1 in. fresh turmeric,
  peeled and chopped (or
  1 teaspoon ground turmeric)

4 macadamia nuts

1 tablespoon shrimp paste

2 teaspoons coriander seeds,
  toasted and ground

TO SERVE

beansprouts, trimmed

½ cucumber, sliced

deep-fried puffed tofu pieces
  or marinated tofu, cubed

crispy fried shallots or onions

fresh coriander/cilantro
  or Vietnamese mint

1 lime, cut into wedges

sambal oelek or chilli oil

SERVES 4

MALAYSIAN CHICKEN LAKSA

Malaysian food draws on its rich heritage of cultures from Chinese to Indian and these combine here to create a truly unique soup. It is always adorned with a selection of garnishes. To speed up preparation time, buy your crispy fried shallots, puffed tofu and sambal oelek chilli paste ready-made from online Asian grocers.

Soak the noodles in a bowlful of hot water for 20–30 minutes until softened. Drain well, shake dry and set aside.

Put the chicken breast in a saucepan with the stock set over a low–medium heat. Simmer very gently for 10 minutes until the chicken is just cooked. Remove the chicken from the stock and set aside to cool completely. Once cool, slice thinly.

To make the laksa paste, pound all the ingredients together using a large pestle and mortar or blitz in a food processor until smooth.

Heat the oil in a wok or non-stick saucepan set over a medium heat and add the laksa paste. Fry for 2 minutes until fragrant, then add the coconut milk and chicken stock. Simmer gently for 10 minutes and then stir in the coconut cream, fish sauce and sugar. Simmer gently for a further 2–3 minutes.

Divide the noodles between serving bowls and add the sliced chicken. Pour over the hot soup and serve topped with a selection of garnishes. Pass around a pot of sambal oelek or chilli oil, to drizzle.

GOAN CHICKEN SOUP WITH SPICED TARKA TOPPING

Indians don't go in for soup – unless it's a remnant of some kind of colonial rule, as this one is. The Portuguese were loath to leave Goa when India gained independence in 1947 and now, Christian Goa is the only place in India that you'll find beef and pork dishes. Chicken, however, is acceptable to everyone except strict vegetarians. Somehow, Indian chickens just taste better than regular chickens, and there is no question that they are free range.

1 tablespoon peanut oil or ghee

1 onion, finely chopped

3 garlic cloves, crushed

3 cm/1¼ in. fresh ginger, peeled and grated

125 g/⅔ cup rice, preferably basmati

½ teaspoon ground turmeric

1 litre/4 cups Chicken Stock (see page 9)

100 g/⅔ cup peas

500 g/1 lb. cooked chicken, shredded into bite-sized pieces

sea salt and freshly ground black pepper

TARKA TOPPING

2 tablespoons peanut oil or ghee

1 tablespoon mustard seeds

2–4 garlic cloves, finely sliced crossways

3 small yellow onions, finely sliced

a handful of curry leaves (optional)

SERVES 4

Heat the oil in a saucepan, add the onion, garlic and ginger and fry gently until softened but not browned. Add the rice, turmeric, salt and pepper and stock.

Simmer for 10 minutes, then add the peas and chicken and simmer until the rice is soft, about another 10 minutes.

To make the tempered topping (a favourite garnish in India), heat the oil in a wok or frying pan/skillet, add the mustard seeds and fry until they pop. Add the garlic and stir-fry until crisp. Take care, because it can easily burn and burnt garlic is bitter. Remove with a slotted spoon and set aside. Add the onions and stir-fry at a low temperature until well covered with oil. Continue cooking until tender. Add the curry leaves, if using, and cook them for a few minutes until aromatic. Return the garlic to the mixture and remove from the heat.

To serve, ladle the soup into bowls, then top with the tempered mixture.

Tip Basmati rice works well in Indian dishes because it is so deliciously fragrant. However, it is the most prized and delicate of rice varieties, and should be handled gently because the grains can easily break.

BEEF GOULASH SOUP WITH SOUR CREAM

olive oil, for frying

100 g/3¾ oz. smoked streaky/
fatty bacon, finely chopped

1 kg/2¼ lb. braising steak or
beef shin, cut into 2.5 cm/
1 in. chunks

2 heaped tablespoons plain/
all-purpose flour

2 large onions, thinly sliced

2 red (bell) peppers, deseeded
and sliced

3 garlic cloves, crushed

5 juniper berries, crushed

2 bay leaves

1 tablespoon sweet smoked
paprika

½ tablespoon hot paprika

2 teaspoons caraway seeds

2 tablespoons tomato purée/
paste

1 tablespoon red wine vinegar

1.2 litres/5 cups Beef Stock
(see page 9)

300 g/11 oz. waxy potatoes,
cut into chunks

2 beetroot/beets, cut into
chunks

sea salt and ground
black pepper

freshly chopped parsley
and sour cream, to serve

SERVES 6

This Hungarian dish is always popular in the mountains, where it makes a hearty meal after an energetic day on the slopes and trails. There is a healthy kick of paprika with the added richness of sour cream, which helps to make this one of the most warming and comforting dishes. This is also delicious made with pork instead of beef – use a slow-cook cut such as shoulder/butt and cut it into large chunks.

Heat a good layer of olive oil in a flameproof casserole or large saucepan and fry the bacon over a medium heat until starting to colour. Remove with a slotted spoon and set aside.

Dust the beef in the flour with plenty of seasoning, then brown in batches over a high heat in the same pan, adding more oil if necessary. Remove and set aside with the bacon.

Add a little more oil to the pan and add the onions and (bell) peppers. Cook for 10 minutes until softened and the onions start to colour. Add the garlic, juniper, bay and spices, and fry for a few minutes before adding the tomato purée/paste, vinegar and stock.

Return the beef and bacon to the pan and season well. Bring to a simmer, then cover and cook for 2–2½ hours until the beef is starting to become really tender.

Add the potatoes and beetroot/beets to the pan and simmer, with the lid off, until the vegetables are tender.

Stir in the parsley and serve in large warmed bowls with generous dollops of sour cream.

NEW ENGLAND CLAM CHOWDER

There are many kinds of chowder – featured here is the New England variety, made with clams and cream and an alternative British kind, made with corn and smoked haddock instead of the clams. There is also a Manhattan kind, made with tomatoes.

2 kg/4 lb. quahog clams, in the shell, or 1 kg/2 lb. smoked haddock

125 ml/½ cup Fish Stock (see page 8) or clam juice, plus extra fish stock to make 1 litre/4 cups

500 g/1 lb. 2 oz. smoked pancetta, cut into cubes

sunflower oil (see method)

3 onions, coarsely chopped

1 celery stalk, chopped

1 carrot, chopped

2 bay leaves

a few sprigs of thyme

250 g/4–5 salad potatoes, peeled and cut into cubes

500 ml/2 cups double/heavy cream

sea salt and freshly cracked black pepper

a large bunch of flat-leaf parsley, coarsely chopped

crackers, to serve

SERVES 4

Put the clams in a large saucepan, then add 125 ml/½ cup of water and the fish stock or clam juice. Cover the pan, bring to the boil and boil hard until the clams open. Remove them as soon as they do and shell over a bowl. Don't overcook or they will be tough. Discard the shells, reserve the clams and return the juice in the bowl to the pan. Strain the cooking liquid through a sieve/strainer, then through muslin/cheesecloth into a measuring jug. Add enough fish stock to make up to 1 litre/4 cups. Taste it and reserve.

Clean the pan, add the bacon and cook slowly to render the fat (add a dash of oil to encourage it if you like – but sunflower, not olive). Remove the crisp bacon and set aside.

Add the onions, celery, carrots, bay leaves and thyme to the saucepan. Cook gently until the onions are softened and translucent. Add the potato cubes and the reserved 1 litre/4 cups stock. Simmer until the potatoes are done, about 10 minutes.

Chop half the clams, and cut the others in half through their thickness. Add the clams, bacon and cream to the saucepan and heat through. Taste and add salt if necessary (remember the clam juices and bacon are already salty). Remove and discard the bay leaves and thyme.

Serve sprinkled with lots of cracked pepper, crisp bacon, handfuls of parsley and crackers.

Note To use smoked haddock instead of clams, put the fish stock and water in a saucepan and bring to the boil. Add the haddock, reduce the heat to a bare simmer and leave until the fish can be flaked. Remove from the liquid and remove the skin from the fish. Discard the skin, put the fish on a plate a flake it into large chunks. Strain the stock.

To make it a British Chowder, add 250 g frozen corn at the same time as the potatoes. Omit the crackers when serving.

ISTRIAN MINESTRONE WITH PEARL BARLEY

The best season to make this minestrone in is early summer, when peas are fresh from the pod and string beans are young and soft. Cooking it with pearl barley makes it chewy and more satisfying, but do go with the more traditional pasta if you prefer.

140 g/5 oz. yellow string beans
    or fresh corn kernels

4 tablespoons olive oil

1 large onion, diced

2 bay leaves

½ teaspoon fennel seeds

½ teaspoon dried basil

1 large carrot, diced

150 g/1 cup peas,
    fresh or frozen

1.2 litres/5 cups water

1½ tablespoons vegetable
    bouillon powder

110 g /½ cup cooked pearl
    barley

30 g/1 cup fennel, spinach
    or other greens

2 garlic cloves, crushed

sea salt and crushed
    black pepper

SERVES 4

Pinch off the tops of the string beans and cut the beans diagonally into 1.5-cm/½-in. pieces. Heat the oil in a large saucepan, add the onion, bay leaves, fennel seeds, dried basil and a pinch of salt and cook for a minute, then add the carrot and stir well. Cook for another minute or two, and repeat the same procedure with the peas and string beans or corn kernels, then stir everything together, cover and cook for about 10 minutes over a low to medium heat.

In another saucepan, bring the water to the boil and keep it warm.

Add the bouillon powder to the sautéed vegetables and stir well. Pour over the boiling water and bring to the boil again. Let cook for 10 minutes, and add the cooked pearled barley or dried pasta and let simmer for another 10 minutes. Add salt and pepper to taste. Chop the spinach (or other greens) and mix it with the crushed garlic in a small bowl. Add this to the minestrone a couple of minutes before serving.

Serve immediately, especially if using pasta, since it soaks up a lot of the soup liquid when left to rest for too long, and you end up with a stew and not a soup!

Tip This minestrone is a great way to use leftover pearl barley, but you can also cook it from scratch.

VIETNAMESE BEEF PHO

In any city with a Vietnamese population, it is worth making a trip to wherever the majority of Vietnamese have settled to seek out an authentic beef pho. It is the large baskets of colourful herbs and condiments give this classic soup its freshness and unique flavour and texture. You need to prepare it a day in advance to allow the flavours to develop.

1 kg/2 lb. beef short ribs

5 cm/2 in. fresh ginger, peeled, sliced and pounded

1 onion, sliced

2 garlic cloves, sliced

3 whole star anise, pounded

2 cinnamon sticks, pounded

400 g/14 oz. dried rice stick noodles

350 g/1⅓ cups thinly sliced beef fillet

3 tablespoons fish sauce

1 teaspoon salt

1 teaspoon caster/granulated sugar

freshly squeezed juice of 1 lime

125 g/2⅓ cups bean sprouts, trimmed

GARNISHES

2 red bird's eye chillies/chiles, chopped

a handful each of fresh Thai basil, Vietnamese mint and coriander/cilantro

6 spring onions/scallions, trimmed and sliced

SERVES 4

Put the ribs in a large saucepan, cover with cold water and bring to the boil. Simmer for 10 minutes then drain and wash the ribs. Return them to the pan and add 2 litres/3½ cups more cold water along with the ginger, onion, garlic, star anise and cinnamon. Return to the boil and simmer gently for 1½ hours, or until the meat is tender.

Carefully remove the ribs from the stock and set aside to cool. Thinly shred the meat, discarding bones. Strain the stock through a fine mesh sieve/strainer and set aside to cool. Refrigerate both the meat and the stock overnight.

The next day, soak the noodles in a bowlful of hot water for 20–30 minutes, until softened. Drain well, shake dry and divide the noodles between large bowls.

Meanwhile, skim and discard the layer of fat from the cold stock and return the pan to a medium heat until just boiling. Stir in the shredded meat, beef fillet, fish sauce, salt, sugar and lime juice. Place the beef fillet on the noodles, spoon over the stock and top with the beansprouts.

Serve with a plate of the garnishes in the middle of the table for everyone to help themselves.

MOROCCAN HARIRA

There are a great many recipes for harira (a rustic spiced soup), traditionally served to break the fast during Ramadan in North Africa, especially in Morocco. The ingredients vary from region to region, but usually include lentils or chickpeas/garbanzos, onions, tomatoes, celery, rice, beaten eggs, fresh herbs such as parsley and coriander/ cilantro, spices like cinnamon, saffron, ginger and black pepper, and often a small amount of whatever meat is to hand. This recipe is really hearty, more a main dish than a prelude of things to come.

3 tablespoons olive oil

1 lamb shank, weighing about 300 g/10 oz.

125 g/½ cup dried chickpeas (garbanzo beans), soaked for 24 hours and drained, or the contents of ½ x 400-g/14-oz. can, drained

125 g/½ cup dried green lentils, rinsed and drained

1 onion, finely chopped

3 celery sticks, trimmed and chopped

½ teaspoon ground cinnamon

1 teaspoon ground turmeric

½ teaspoon ground ginger

1 teaspoon saffron strands

1 tablespoon tomato purée/paste

2 tablespoons plain/ all-purpose flour

3 tablespoons chopped fresh flat-leaf parsley

4 tablespoons chopped fresh coriander/cilantro

salt and ground black pepper

lemon quarters, to serve

SERVES 6

Heat the oil in a large saucepan (a capacity of 2 litres/8½ cups) and brown the lamb on all sides. Add the chickpeas/garbanzos, lentils, onion, celery, spices and tomato purée/paste to the saucepan, then pour in 1.5 litres/6½ cups of water. Stir well. Cover the pan and bring to the boil, then after 10 minutes turn down the heat and simmer everything together for 1½–2 hours, until the chickpeas/garbanzos are tender and the meat is falling off the bone.

Remove the lamb shank from the soup and strip the meat off the bone, then chop the meat and return it to the saucepan.

Whisk the flour into 300 ml/1¼ cups of cold water, blending until it is completely smooth, then stir the mixture into the soup. Bring the soup back to the boil and simmer for 10 minutes to thicken the broth.

Stir in the chopped fresh herbs, season with salt and plenty of black pepper and serve with lemon quarters to squeeze in the soup.

Tip While it may seem odd to Europeans, dates or dried figs are often offered with the soup, or even honey cakes, but bread would be a good savoury substitute if that idea doesn't appeal.

LONDON PARTICULAR

This soup has a curious history. Don't let the name put you off what is truly a delightful soup made with dried split peas. It refers to the dense, greenish smog – known initially as a 'pea-souper', but later as a 'London Particular' – that frequently plagued London from the start of the Industrial Revolution in the late 18th century until the introduction of the Clean Air Act in 1956. If the ham hock is very salty, soak it in water overnight before using, and discard the water.

30 g/2 tablespoons butter

1 onion, chopped

1 celery stick, trimmed and chopped

1 large carrot, peeled and chopped

400 g/2 cups dried green or yellow split peas, preferably soaked overnight and drained

1 small ham hock (approximately 500 g/1 lb.)

salt and ground black pepper

SERVES 4

Melt the butter in a large saucepan and fry the onion, celery and carrot until soft. Add the drained split peas to the pan, together with the ham hock and 1.8 litres/7½ cups of water. Cover and bring to the boil, then turn down the heat and simmer for about 2½ hours, or until the meat is falling off the bone and the peas are breaking down into the liquid.

Remove the ham hock from the pan, strip off the skin, gristle and fat, lift the meat off the bone and cut into bite-size chunks.

If you like the soup smooth, blend it to a purée using a blender, then return it to the pan, add the ham and reheat. Otherwise, just return the ham chunks to the pan, season to taste and serve.

Ingredients

2 tablespoons vegetable oil

1 large onion, finely chopped

1 teaspoon cumin seeds

1 teaspoon ground coriander

1 teaspoon chilli powder

2 garlic cloves, finely chopped

½ x 400-g/14-oz. can chopped tomatoes

950 ml/4 cups water

425 g/15 oz. black beans

2 teaspoons freshly squeezed lime juice

1 tablespoon chopped coriander/cilantro

sea salt and freshly ground black pepper, to taste

CHIA SEED CREAM

1 tablespoon chia seeds

4 tablespoons crème fraîche

1 teaspoon freshly squeezed lime juice

a pinch of sea salt

SERVES 4

BLACK BEAN & TOMATO SOUP
WITH LIME & CHIA SEED CREAM

There is nothing wrong with using canned beans to create a super, fresh tasting, easy dinner. Hiding a super seed in the salsa adds a stealthy extra health punch, too!

For the chia seed cream garnish, toss all the ingredients in a bowl and chill in the refrigerator while you make the soup so the chia seeds expand.

Heat the oil in a frying pan/skillet and fry the onion, cumin seeds, coriander and chilli powders over a medium heat for 5–8 minutes until the onions are translucent. Add the garlic and fry for a minute longer. Reserve a few beans and tomatoes for serving, then add the chopped tomatoes, water and black beans and stir. Reduce the temperature, cover and cook for 15 minutes. Set aside to cool.

Once cooled, purée the soup in a food processor. Adjust the seasoning if required. Return to the heat and warm through. Serve in bowls, with the reserved beans and tomatoes, a squeeze of lime juice (about a teaspoon each) and garnish with fresh coriander/cilantro and a dollop of the chia garnish.

LUXURIOUS SOUPS

GAME CONSOMMÉ
WITH SOFTLY BOILED QUAILS' EGGS & BRIOCHE

400 g/14 oz. minced/
  ground chicken

2 onions, diced

1 leek, sliced

2 celery sticks, sliced

1 garlic clove, chopped

4 egg whites

4 litres/quarts game stock
  (follow the recipe for Beef
  Stock on page 9, using duck,
  pigeon, pheasant, partridge
  and venison bones, or a
  mixture)

12 juniper berries, slightly
  crushed to release their
  flavour

a good sprig of fresh thyme

2 bay leaves

2 tablespoons tomato
  purée/paste

a splash of dry sherry, to taste

sea salt and ground
  black pepper

TO SERVE

8 slices of brioche, buttered
  on both sides and sliced
  into fingers

8 quails' or gulls' eggs

a small pot of pâté de foie gras
  (optional)

a deep, narrow stock pan

*a muslin/cheesecloth-lined
  sieve/strainer or jelly bag*

SERVES 8

Consommé is always special and here, the addition of quails' eggs and brioche makes the effort it takes to make worthwhile.

Put the chicken, all the vegetables and the garlic in the bowl of a food processor and pulse into a rough paste. In a mixing bowl, gently whisk the egg whites to loosen them and create bubbles. Add the egg white to the chicken mixture and blitz for a further 3 seconds only. Transfer to a bowl, cover and chill for 10 minutes.

Pour the stock into the stock pan and add the juniper berries, thyme, bay leaves and tomato purée/paste. Bring the liquid to the boil, then reduce to a simmer. Add the chicken mixture and incorporate it evenly into the stock with a balloon whisk. Bring the liquid to the boil and keep it at a steady rolling boil until the liquid has reduced to half the volume. During cooking, a white crust with a dirty, silty look to it will form on top of the liquid. Small holes will appear in the crust, being forced open by the heat and steam of the stock beneath. Towards the end of the simmering time, very carefully prise open one of the holes in the crust to check that the liquid beneath is clear. When satisfied that the clarity has been achieved, carefully lift the crust off the liquid with a large slotted spoon. Strain the consommé through the muslin/cheesecloth-lined sieve/strainer into a clean pan. When ready to serve the consommé, heat it through very gently (don't let it boil or it will go cloudy), add a good splash of dry sherry and season with salt and black pepper.

Preheat the oven to 190°C (375°F) Gas 5. Lay the buttered brioche slices on a baking sheet and bake in the oven for 5–7 minutes, until crisp and golden.

To boil the quails' eggs, pop them in a pan of cold water and set over medium heat. When the water reaches simmering point, draw the pan off the heat and leave the eggs to sit in the hot water for 1 minute. Drain off the water and gently peel the eggs.

Ladle the soup into tureens and pop a boiled quails' egg into each one. Serve with the hot toasted buttered brioche and pâté de foie gras, if wished.

ALE, CARAMELIZED ONION & THYME SOUP

French onion soup is normally made using an Alpine white wine, but this version, popular in British pubs, uses ale instead. It is buttery and sweet, but with the bitter balance of a good full-flavoured strong ale.

40 g/3 tablespoons butter

3 large onions, finely sliced

2 large garlic cloves, crushed

20 g/2 tablespoons dark muscovado/dark brown sugar

200 ml/¾ cup ale

800 ml/3⅓ cups Beef Stock (see page 9)

2 tablespoons Dijon mustard

3 sprigs of fresh thyme

a handful of fresh parsley, chopped

sea salt and ground black pepper

FOR THE ROUX (OPTIONAL)

30 g/2 tablespoons butter

1 tablespoon plain/ all-purpose flour

TO SERVE

6 slices of baguette

olive oil, for brushing

grated Gruyère cheese, or other strong hard cheese

SERVES 6

Melt the butter in a heavy-based saucepan, add the finely sliced onions and cook over gentle heat until very soft and reduced in volume. They need to be silky, and with no resistance at all – this will take about 20–25 minutes. Add the garlic and brown sugar and cook for a few more minutes to allow the onions to take on a deep golden colour, but do not let them crisp.

Pour over the ale and stock, then add the mustard and fresh thyme. If your thyme is of the 'stalky' variety, pick off as many of the little leaves as possible, but add the stalks to impart their flavour, and pull them out before you serve. If you are using soft summer thyme, roughly chop and add it all. Simmer for about 10 minutes to allow all the flavours to infuse. By this time, the onions should be as soft as butter and have no resistance to the bite.

To thicken the soup a little, make a roux. Gently melt the butter in a small saucepan, then remove the pan from the heat and stir in the flour. A little at a time, add the roux mixture to the simmering soup, stirring all the time to prevent lumps. This will gradually thicken the soup just enough for it to be slightly syrupy. (It is not a thick soup, but the roux adds texture and makes it slightly more hearty. If you are cooking for someone who doesn't eat wheat, it can be left out altogether.) Season the soup with salt and plenty of freshly ground black pepper, then stir in the freshly chopped parsley.

Preheat the oven to 180°C (350°F) Gas 4. Brush the baguette slices with a little olive oil and bake until golden brown.

Ladle the soup into heatproof bowls, place a slice of the baked bread on top and scatter with a generous amount of Gruyère. Place under a hot grill/broiler to melt the cheese, then serve.

WATERCRESS SOUP WITH NASHI PEAR, SCALLOPS & PANCETTA

The very crunchy texture of Nashi pears (also sometimes known as Asian pears and apple pears) contrasts beautifully with the soft richness of scallops. Team this winning combination with the unique flavour of watercress, and you have one very classy soup, perfect for entertaining in style.

50 g/3½ tablespoons butter

6 shallots, finely sliced

2 standard pears, peeled, cored and diced

1.75 litres/7⅓ cups Vegetable Stock (see page 8)

2 big bunches of watercress, well chopped

400 ml/1⅔ cups double/ heavy cream

sea salt and ground black pepper

FOR THE GARNISH

8 slices of pancetta

8 king scallops

1 tablespoon butter

2 Nashi pears

a baking sheet, lined with baking paper

SERVES 6

Melt the butter in a large saucepan and add the shallots and pears. Sauté for 4–5 minutes to soften, but do not allow to colour. Pour in the stock, bring to a simmer and cook for about 8 minutes, until the shallots and pears are tender. Add the watercress and use a spatula to push it down until it is submerged in the liquid and wilted a little (cook for no more than 2 minutes longer so that it retains its vivid green), then draw the pan off the heat. Whizz the soup with a stick blender until very smooth, then pour into a clean pan, stir in the cream and season with salt and pepper.

For the garnish, preheat the oven to 190°C (375°F) Gas 5. Lay the slices of pancetta on the prepared baking sheet and bake in the preheated oven for about 10 minutes, until crisp, being careful not to let them burn. Set aside until needed.

Prepare the scallops by removing any membrane and wiping with paper towels. Leave the corals on, if you wish, or remove them for a cleaner look. Slice the scallops in half horizontally.

Melt the butter in a heavy-based frying pan and sauté the scallops very quickly (they will not need more than 1 minute on each side) until golden. Be careful not to burn the butter, as this will dirty the scallops. Remove them from the pan and set aside.

Peel the Nashi pears, quarter them, then cut each quarter in half again lengthways. Add the pear slices to the pan you have used to fry the scallops and sauté them for a few minutes, until caramelized and golden on both sides.

Ladle the soup into large flat soup bowls and garnish with the scallops, pear slices and a long shard of crisp pancetta.

WINTER SQUASH SOUP
WITH CEP MUSHROOMS & TRUFFLE OIL

This is a deliciously rich and smooth soup with a colour of deep vibrant gold. The silky nature of the cep works so well with the smooth soup. The addition of truffle oil finishes this off and elevates it from the everyday to something really special – but this is at your discretion.

50 g/3½ tablespoons butter

2 white onions, diced

2 garlic cloves, finely chopped

1 small pumpkin, peeled, deseeded and diced

½ butternut squash, peeled, deseeded and diced

1.5 litres/6 cups Vegetable Stock (see page 8)

2 cep mushrooms, finely sliced

200 ml/¾ cup double/ heavy cream

sea salt and ground black pepper

FOR THE GARNISH

truffle oil, for drizzling (optional)

chopped fresh parsley

fresh thyme leaves

SERVES 6

Melt about three-quarters of the butter in a large saucepan and cook the onions, garlic, pumpkin and squash until soft. Add the stock to the pan and bring to the boil. Reduce the heat and simmer for about 15 minutes, until the pumpkin and squash are cooked. Take the pan off the heat and blitz the mixture to a purée with a stick blender.

In a frying pan, heat the remaining butter and fry the ceps very gently for a few minutes, until softened but without colouring. Add the ceps to the soup and stir in the cream, then season to taste with salt and black pepper. Ladle the soup into bowls and serve garnished with a sprinkle of fresh parsley and thyme leaves and a little drizzle of truffle oil, if you wish.

CITRUS BROTH WITH KING PRAWNS, CHILLI & GINGER

FOR THE BROTH

2 litres/quarts Chicken or Fish Stock (see pages 8–9)

6 lemongrass stalks, bashed to release their flavour

2 red chillies/chiles, split (seeds and all)

6 fresh kaffir lime leaves

1 tablespoon sliced fresh ginger

8 spring onions/scallions, sliced

FOR THE SOUP

2–3 tablespoons ground nut oil

500 g/1 lb. 2 oz. raw green king prawns/jumbo shrimp, shelled

3 garlic cloves, finely sliced

1 tablespoon very finely sliced fresh ginger

1 green chill/chilei, finely diced

1 red chilli/chile, finely diced

250 g/9 oz. straw or mixed exotic Chinese mushrooms, finely sliced

2 fresh kaffir lime leaves

10 spring onions/scallions, whites and greens separated, sliced

4–5 tablespoons fish sauce

1–2 tablespoons soy sauce

freshly squeezed juice of 1 lime

a small bunch of fresh coriander/cilantro, leaves only

200 g/7 oz. mange tout/ snow peas or sugar snap peas, sliced on the angle

sea salt and ground black pepper

lime wedges, to serve

SERVES 6

This is such a fresh and healthy broth, it almost does you good just to read the recipe! It will give you a glow in your cheeks and leave you feeling energized and ready to go. You can try it with any other shellfish, too, or scallops or firm white fish would also be delicious. If you cannot find straw mushrooms, use shiitake or another variety of Chinese mushroom – the weirder they look, the better the soup will look!

To make the broth, put all the broth ingredients in a large saucepan and bring the liquid to a simmer. Continue to simmer for 15 minutes or so with the pan covered until an aromatic infusion has been achieved, then pass the broth through a sieve/strainer to remove the seasonings. Set the broth aside until required.

Heat the oil in a large saucepan and add the prawns/shrimp along with the garlic, ginger, green and red chillies/chiles and mushrooms. Toss around until all are well coated in the oil and cook for about 3–5 minutes, until the prawns/shrimp are beginning to turn pink. Pour over the broth, then add the lime leaves, spring onion/scallion whites, fish sauce and soy sauce, and simmer for a further 3–5 minutes.

Add most of the lime juice, taste and then add more lime juice or soy sauce if you feel the seasoning is not sufficient. When happy with the flavour - the soup should be hot, salty and sour - stir in the coriander/cilantro, spring onion/scallion greens and sugar snap peas.

Ladle generous servings of the broth into bowls and serve with lime wedges on the side.

RAMEN BOWLS WITH TEMPURA PRAWNS

Like all Japanese dishes it is the contrast of textures and flavours that defines this dish.
The soft slurp of noodles is balanced with the crisp tempura batter which, once submerged
into the hot stock, becomes soft, gooey and comforting to eat.

8 large prawns/shrimp

1.5 litres/2½ pints Dashi broth made from dashi broth powder

125 ml/½ cup Japanese soy sauce

75 ml/scant ⅓ cup mirin

250 g/9 oz. dried ramen noodles

125 g/2 handfuls mange-tout/snow peas, trimmed and thinly sliced

2 tablespoons dried wakame seaweed

150 g/1 cup plus 1 tablespoon cubed firm tofu

2 large spring onions/ scallions, trimmed and thinly sliced

vegetable oil, for deep-frying

TEMPURA BATTER

1 egg yolk

250 ml/1 cup iced water

100 g/¾ cup plain/all-purpose flour

2 tablespoons potato (or rice) flour

SERVES 4

Peel the prawns/shrimp, leaving the tail section intact and reserving the shells and head. Cut down the back of each one and pull out the black intestinal tract. Wash and dry the prawns/shrimp and set aside. Put the shells and heads in a saucepan set over a medium heat and pour in the broth. Bring to the boil, cover and simmer for 30 minutes. Strain through a fine mesh sieve/strainer and return the stock to the pan. Add the soy sauce and mirin and set aside.

Plunge the noodles into a saucepan of boiling water and cook for about 4 minutes, or until al dente. Drain, refresh under cold water and shake dry.

Set aside.

To make the tempura batter, put the egg yolk, iced water and both flours in a large mixing bowl. Very lightly beat the mixture together using a fork to make a slightly lumpy but thin batter.

Return the broth mixture to a simmer, add the mange-tout/snow peas and seaweed and simmer for 2 minutes. Add the noodles and cook for 1 minute to heat through.

Meanwhile heat about 5 cm/2 in. of oil in a wok or old saucepan until a cube of bread dropped into the oil crisps and turns brown in 20–30 seconds. Dip the prawns/shrimp into the tempura batter, shaking off any excess. Fry in batches for 2–3 minutes until crisp and golden. Carefully remove the cooked prawns/shrimp and drain on paper towels. Add a little of the remaining tempura batter to the oil and cook until crisp. Drain this and put with the prawns/shrimp.

Divide the noodles between warmed soup bowls, add the tofu and spring onions/scallions, then pour over the soup. Top each with two tempura prawns/shrimp and sprinkle the crispy batter bits into the soup. Serve at once.

CALLALOO WITH SORREL & CRAB

250 g/9 oz. white crab meat

grated zest and freshly squeezed juice of 1½ limes

150 g/5½ oz. fresh sorrel leaves, finely sliced

25 g/2 tablespoons salted butter

1 onion, finely sliced

3 garlic cloves, crushed

175 g/6 oz. okra, sliced

2 red chillies/chiles, finely sliced into strips

1.25 litres/5 cups Fish Stock (see page 8)

250 g/9 oz. brown crab meat

a 400-g/14-oz. can coconut milk or a 250-g/9-oz. pack coconut cream

a dash of soy sauce, to taste

a dash of fish sauce, to taste

1 green chilli/chile, finely sliced, or a pinch of chilli powder (optional)

250 g/9 oz. baby spinach leaves

5 spring onions/scallions, finely sliced into strips

½ sweet red (bell) pepper, finely sliced

a dash of double/heavy cream (optional)

sea salt and ground black pepper

grated nutmeg, to garnish

SERVES 6

Callaloo soup, generally made with a bitter green leaf similar to spinach, is very popular in the Caribbean. In this version, the sorrel gives the bitter note while the spinach is a little kinder. The crab is clean and fresh and gives a lovely sweetness against the bitter notes of the leaves. You can use courgette/zucchini instead of okra; if you do cut down the simmering time to about 7–10 minutes.

Put the white crab meat, lime zest and sorrel in a small bowl with a squeeze of the lime juice to 'loosen' the mixture, and leave in the fridge until needed.

Melt the butter in a large saucepan and add the onion, garlic and okra. Sauté for a few minutes, until just soft, then add the red chillies/chiles, stock and brown crab meat. Simmer very gently for 15–20 minutes, until the okra is tender. (The okra will very slightly thicken the soup.) Add the coconut milk or cream and stir until all lumps are incorporated.

This is the best stage to season the soup, and even though there are other fairly punchy ingredients still to come, it is at its most robust at this point. Add a splash each of soy sauce and fish sauce and the remaining lime juice. If you would like a little more heat, add the fresh green chilli/chile (to give better flavour and more subtle heat) or a pinch of chilli powder. When you are happy with the balance of heat, salt (from the soy) and acid (from the lime), add the fresh spinach. When the spinach is wilted, add the spring onions/scallions and red (bell) pepper and cook for a couple of minutes. Finally, stir in the white crab meat mixture and the cream, if using.

Spoon the callaloo into generous bowls and serve with a dusting of grated nutmeg on top for a truly Caribbean finish.

LOBSTER BISQUE

2 large cooked lobsters (if home-cooked, keep the boiling water for stock)

150 g/1¼ sticks butter

2 onions, diced

4 small potatoes, peeled and diced

1 fennel bulb, sliced

4 celery sticks, sliced

1 large leek, white only, sliced

4 garlic cloves, crushed

a 2.5-cm/1-inch piece of fresh ginger, peeled and grated, or a good pinch of ground ginger (optional)

2 bay leaves

2 sprigs of fresh tarragon or 1 generous teaspoon dried

2 litres/quarts Fish Stock (make it with the lobster poaching water, if home-cooked – see page 8)

200 g/7 oz. fresh or canned chopped tomatoes

200 ml/¾ cup white wine

4 tablespoons tomato purée/paste

150 ml/⅔ cup vermouth plus 150 ml/⅔ cup Cognac, or 300 ml/1¼ cups of either

a good pinch of cayenne pepper

a dash of Tabasco (optional)

250 g/1 cup double/heavy cream, plus a little extra to garnish

a squeeze of lemon juice, to taste

sea salt and ground black pepper

freshly snipped chives, to garnish

SERVES 6

This bisque is the epitome of decadence – lobster with cream and brandy. It's not an everyday dish, but definitely one to prepare once in a while, for very special occasions. Every cook should have a recipe for when that moment comes – and here it is... If you like, you can cheat and replace one of the lobsters with some white and dark crab meat, adding the meat just before serving.

Remove all the meat from the cooked lobster tails and claws, and set aside. Reserve the shells to flavour the soup.

Melt the butter in a large saucepan and add all the vegetables, garlic, ginger and herbs, then add the lobster shells. Pour in the stock, tomatoes and white wine, cover the pan and leave to simmer gently with the lid on for about 1 hour.

Now, some people liquidize the shell and all, but if you worry about the sharpness of the blade on your stick blender, remove the shells from the pan, and blend all the other bits until smooth. If brave, and you have strong blades, you can whizz the lot! Pass the soup through a fine-meshed sieve/strainer twice, using a ladle to force the purée through to achieve a fine smooth base. Pour the soup into a clean pan and stir in the tomato purée/paste.

Put the vermouth and Cognac in a separate small pan and set over high heat. Very carefully flambé the liquid by using a long kitchen match to set the alcohol alight. Simply touch a lit match to the very edge of the pan and the alcohol fumes will catch – stand well back! The flames will die down once all the alcohol has burned away. When this has happened, pour the remaining liquid into the soup.

Add the cayenne pepper and a little splash of Tabasco, if you like it hot. Stir in the cream and a squeeze of lemon juice to lift the flavour, then season with salt and black pepper. Lastly, and just before you want to eat it, gently warm the soup to a simmer and add the reserved lobster meat to heat through.

Serve the soup in elegant bowls, garnished with a swirl of cream and snipped chives.

MUSSEL & FISH SOUP WITH ROUILLE

2 whole red mullet, gutted

120 ml/½ cup olive oil

1.5 kg/3 lb. 5 oz. mussels, cleaned and bearded

2 leeks (whites only), finely sliced

1 large strong onion, finely diced

1 fennel bulb, finely sliced

2 garlic cloves, chopped

2 red (bell) peppers, deseeded and finely sliced

a good pinch of saffron fronds

6 large ripe tomatoes, diced

2.5 litres/quarts fish or Vegetable Stock (see page 8)

2 bay leaves

a small bunch of fresh thyme

a small bunch of fresh parsley, plus extra, chopped, to garnish

2 large pieces of orange zest (pared with a potato peeler to avoid pith)

2–3 tablespoons tomato purée/paste

110 g/2¼ cups white breadcrumbs

75 ml/5 tablespoons Pastis (or Pernod)

sea salt and ground black pepper

FOR THE ROUILLE

6 garlic cloves, crushed

1 egg yolk

1–2 teaspoons cayenne pepper

150 ml/⅔ cup olive oil

SERVES 6

Close your eyes and you'll be transported to Brittany by this wonderfully powerful soup. The authentically French fennel and Pastis bring it to life and it is worth the effort required to make it.

Descale the red mullet and make sure it is cleaned well. Roughly chop the fish into large pieces, keeping the head and fins on.

Heat the oil in a large pan, toss in the mussels and place a lid firmly over the pan. Cook over high heat for 1 minute, then, holding the lid down firmly, shake the pan to toss the mussels. Cook for a further 2 minutes, then toss once more. Remove the lid and all the mussels should be open (discard any that haven't opened). Using a slotted spoon, remove the mussels from the pan, leaving the oil and any liquor from the mussels in the pan.

Add the leeks and onion to the pan and cook gently to soften without browning, then add the fennel, garlic, peppers, saffron and tomatoes. Cover with the stock and add the red mullet pieces, herbs and orange zest. Bring the liquid to the boil, then stir in the tomato purée/paste and the breadcrumbs. Reduce the heat and simmer the soup, uncovered, for about 15 minutes.

In the meantime, remove the mussels from their shells, leaving a few in the shells to garnish.

Set a fine-meshed sieve/strainer over another large pan and pass the soup through the sieve/strainer, pushing all the fish, breadcrumbs and vegetables through the mesh to get as much texture from the solids as possible. You will now have a fishy, slightly thick soup. (If you would like it to be smoother, blend briefly with a stick blender.) Season well with salt and pepper, then stir in the mussels, Pastis and freshly chopped parsley.

To make the rouille, put the garlic in a blender with the egg yolk and a pinch of salt and blend until smooth. Gradually add the oil, a trickle at a time, until it is all incorporated and a good thick cream is achieved. Add the cayenne pepper, to taste.

Serve the soup in large flat bowls, garnished with the reserved mussels in their shells, with the rouille and French crusty bread.

PHEASANT SOUP WITH MUSHROOMS & PORT

FOR THE MARINADE

500 ml/2 cups ruby Port

2 red onions, finely chopped

2 garlic cloves, crushed

2 bay leaves

a few sprigs of fresh thyme

6 juniper berries, slightly
crushed to release their
flavour

FOR THE SOUP

1 large pheasant, skinned
and jointed

50–75 g/3½–5 tablespoons
butter

1.5 litres/6 cups game stock
(follow the recipe for Beef
Stock on page 9, using duck,
pigeon, pheasant, partridge
and venison bones, or a
mixture)

500 g/1 lb. 2 oz. chestnut,
shiitake or button
mushrooms, or a mixture

1 tablespoon cornflour/
cornstarch

2 egg yolks

250 ml/1 cup double/
heavy cream

sea salt and ground
black pepper

croutons, to serve

*a large flameproof
casserole dish*

SERVES 6–8

This recipe is named for a lady called Annabel who claimed not
to be able to cook. Her signature pheasant dish was the inspiration
for this deliciously rich soup, and as you'll see if you make it, this
soup proves how wrong that claim of incompetence was!

Combine all the marinade ingredients in a dish and add
the pheasant joints. Make sure all the meat is covered in the
marinade and leave for 8 hours or overnight in the fridge.

When ready to make the soup, remove the pheasant joints
from the marinade and dry thoroughly with paper towels.
Reserve the marinade.

Heat 1–2 tablespoons of the butter in the casserole dish and
cook the joints until nicely browned. Pour over the reserved
marinade, along with the game stock. Set the dish over low
heat and poach the pheasant very gently for 1½ hours.

Remove the pheasant joints from the liquid (reserving the liquid)
and allow to cool. Shred all the meat from the bones, being
careful that all the bones are removed. Set the meat aside.

Heat the remaining butter in a frying pan and sauté the
mushrooms gently, giving a little colour, then set aside.

Strain the poaching liquid, discarding the bits, and pour it into
a clean pan. Bring the liquid to a very gentle simmer, then add
the shredded meat and mushrooms.

In a small bowl, combine the cornflour/cornstarch, egg yolks
and cream and mix to a smooth paste. Stir the mixture into the
simmering liquid and allow to just thicken, then draw the pan
off the heat. Season with salt and black pepper.

Ladle the soup into bowls and serve with old-fashioned
croutons on the side.

GUINEA FOWL RISOTTO SOUP
WITH PORCINI MUSHROOMS, PUMPKIN & THYME

Guinea fowl is a superb eating bird, far superior in flavour to chicken, and less polarizing than other stronger game birds. Here, in this satisfying, soupy risotto, it is succulent, full-flavoured and delicious.

100 g/3½ oz. dried porcini mushrooms

1 guinea fowl

1 onion, diced

1 carrot, peeled and diced

2 celery sticks, diced

a bunch of fresh thyme, plus leaves from another small bunch

4 garlic cloves, 1 bashed and 3 crushed

½ small pumpkin, peeled, deseeded and diced

100 ml/7 tablespoons olive oil

2 red onions, diced

250 g/1¼ cups Arborio risotto rice

600 g/1 lb. 5 oz. mixed fresh mushrooms, including shiitake, sliced

15 g/1 tablespoon butter

100 ml/7 tablespoons white wine

a small bunch of fresh parsley, chopped

a squeeze of lemon juice, to taste

200 g/2 cups freshly grated Parmesan cheese

sea salt and ground black pepper

SERVES 6–8

Soak the dried porcini mushrooms in a little water for at least 1 hour. Once rehydrated, drain (reserve the soaking water) and chop down any very large mushrooms.

Put the guinea fowl in a large saucepan and add the onion, carrot, celery, bunch of thyme and the bashed garlic clove. Pour over 2 litres/quarts water, set the pan over medium heat and bring to a simmer. Poach the guinea fowl very gently for about 1½ hours, until it is cooked and very tender, and the meat is falling off the bone. Remove the bird from the pan and strain the liquid, reserving the stock to use later. Once the guinea fowl is cool, strip all the flesh from the carcass and set aside.

Preheat the oven to 190°C (375°F) Gas 5.

Put the diced pumpkin in a large roasting pan and drizzle with a little of the olive oil. Roast in the preheated oven for 15–20 minutes, until tender and golden.

Heat the remaining oil in large heavy-based saucepan, add the red onions and crushed garlic and cook for a few minutes, until softened. Add the rice, stir to coat in the oil and cook for a further minute, then add the rehydrated porcini, sliced fresh mushrooms and the butter. Cook until the mushrooms have wilted, then pour in the reserved guinea fowl stock and porcini soaking water. Simmer, stirring often, for about 12–15 minutes, until the rice is almost cooked, adding more water if needed – the soup should be thick, but loose enough to spoon into a bowl. When the rice is almost tender, add the shredded meat, roast pumpkin and white wine and cook for 2 more minutes, until the rice is perfectly cooked and the meat and pumpkin have warmed.

Season with salt and pepper and add the parsley and thyme leaves, then lift the flavour with a squeeze of lemon juice. Lastly, stir in half of the Parmesan and serve the soup with remainder on the side, for sprinkling.

Ingredients

4 tablespoons vegetable oil
 or ghee

2 onions, finely sliced

750 g–1 kg/1¾–2¼ lbs. lamb
 (leg, rump or shoulder),
 cut into bite-size pieces

2 garlic cloves, crushed

2 red chillies/chiles, deseeded
 and sliced

a 2.5-cm/1-inch piece of fresh
 ginger, peeled and grated

½ tablespoon ground cumin

1½ tablespoons garam masala

½ tablespoon ground coriander

about 1 teaspoon chilli powder

2 teaspoons ground turmeric

8 green cardamom pods

1 teaspoon ground cloves

1 litre/4 cups Chicken
 or Vegetable Stock
 (see pages 8–9)

a 400-ml/14-oz. can
 coconut milk

250 ml/1 cup passata
 (Italian sieved tomatoes)

200 g/1 cup red or green lentils

a squeeze of lemon juice

500 g/1 lb. baby spinach leaves

sea salt and ground
 black pepper

a handful of fresh coriander/
 cilantro, roughly chopped

100 g/1 cup flaked/slivered
 almonds, toasted

FOR THE RAITA

a bunch of fresh mint leaves,
 finely chopped

200 g/¾ cup plain yogurt
 (sheeps' milk is best)

½ cucumber, grated

SERVES 6–8

CREAMY COCONUT & LAMB SOUP
WITH CUMIN, CARDAMOM & ALMONDS

Indian food is an absolute celebration of intriguing spices and flavours. This simple but delicious soup celebrates that, and is wonderful served with warm naan breads and the raita.

Heat the oil in a large heavy-based saucepan and add the onions and lamb. Cook over medium–high heat until the lamb is sealed and turning an even brown. Add the garlic, chilli/chile, ginger and all the dried spices and continue to cook over medium heat for a further few minutes, until the lamb has taken up all the spices.

Pour on the stock, coconut milk and passata, cover the pan and cook very gently for 40–50 minutes, until the lamb is almost tender. Stir in the lentils and continue cooking over low heat for a further 15 minutes, until the soup is thickened and the lentils are cooked. Season with salt and pepper, and add a little more chilli powder if you would like more heat. Finally, lift the flavour with a little lemon juice.

To make the raita, stir together the mint, yogurt and cucumber.

Just before serving, gently stir the baby spinach leaves into the soup, to wilt them, then ladle the piping hot soup into large soup plates. Scatter the coriander/cilantro leaves and the almonds over the bowls and serve with the raita on the side (or you can swirl a little into the soup, if preferred).

DIM SUM DUCK WONTON SOUP

Chinese BBQ duck is considered somewhat clichéd, but that doesn't stop it from being absolutely delicious if done well, of course. Here, to add a little fun to this soup, the duck, spring onions/scallions, cucumber and hoisin sauce form the filling for wontons. And the skin is deep fried to add a fabulous bite to the finished soup.

½ cooked Chinese BBQ duck

1 small onion, roughly chopped

5 cm/2 in. fresh ginger, peeled, sliced and pounded

4 garlic cloves

3 whole star anise, lightly bruised

1 cinnamon stick, lightly bruised

75 ml/scant ⅓ cup shaoxing rice wine

75 ml/scant ⅓ cup dark soy sauce

½ cucumber, deseeded and finely chopped

2 large spring onions/scallions, trimmed and finely chopped

2 tablespoons hoisin sauce

1 egg, beaten

24 wonton wrappers

vegetable oil, for deep frying

2 pak choi/bok choy, trimmed and thickly sliced

1 tablespoon chopped fresh coriander/cilantro

TO SERVE

crispy duck skin

coriander/cilantro leaves

SERVES 4

Remove the skin and meat from the duck and place the bones in a saucepan with 2 litres/3½ pints of cold water. Add the onion, ginger, garlic, star anise and cinnamon stick and bring to the boil over a medium heat. Partially cover the pan and simmer gently for 30 minutes. Strain the stock through a fine mesh sieve/strainer into a clean saucepan and stir in the shaoxing and soy sauce.

Meanwhile, chop the duck meat and put in a bowl with the cucumber, spring onions/scallions and hoisin sauce. Add half the beaten egg and mix to combine.

Working one at a time, lay the wonton wrappers out flat and place a tablespoon of the duck filling in the middle of each. Brush the edges with the remaining beaten egg and press together to seal.

Heat about 5 cm/2 in. oil in a wok or old saucepan until a cube of bread dropped into the oil crisps and turns brown in 20–30 seconds. Cut the duck skin into thin strips and fry in the hot oil until crispy. Remove from the pan and drain on paper towels.

Bring the duck stock to a gentle simmer, add the wontons and cook for 5 minutes. Remove with a slotted spoon and divide between serving bowls.

Add the pak choi/bok choy to the stock and simmer for 2–3 minutes until tender. Divide the pak choi/bok choy between the bowls and pour over the stock.

Serve the soup with the crispy duck skin and a few coriander/cilantro leaves sprinkled on top.

WILD GARLIC & NETTLE SOUP
WITH A POACHED EGG

Nettles and wild garlic/ramps are a traditional spring combination and they make a delicious soup. Use an old pair of gloves when picking nettles to protect your hands but don't worry about eating them, 30 seconds in boiling water is all it takes to remove the sting.

4 carrots, peeled and finely diced

2 onions, finely diced

2 celery sticks, sliced

leaves of 2–3 large bunches of wild nettles (available in health food stores, at farmers' markets or online, see Note)

12 wild garlic/ramp leaves

4 eggs

150 g/1¼ cup grated Gruyère cheese

table salt freshly ground black pepper, to season

SERVES 4

Put the carrots, onions and celery in a large saucepan with 2 litres/quarts of water. Set over a medium heat and bring to a low simmer for 30 minutes. Add the nettles and wild garlic/ramp and simmer for a further 20 minutes.

Purée the soup using a handheld electric blender to form a smooth liquid. Keep warm.

In a separate pan, cook the poached eggs. First, place the whole egg (shell on) in a saucepan of simmering water for 10 seconds, then plunge it in a bowl of cold water until it's cool enough to touch. Add a few drops of vinegar to the pan of simmering water, crack in the eggs. You may need to do this in batches depending on the size of your pan. Cook the eggs for 3 minutes each then lift from the water using a slotted spoon. Carefully lay the eggs on paper towels to drain off any excess water.

Preheat the grill/broiler to hot.

Ladle the soup into warm bowls. Gently, place a poached egg on top of the soup and sprinkle the Gruyère cheese over. Set the bowls under the hot grill/broiler until the cheese is golden. Serve immediately sprinkled with black pepper.

Note Wild nettles can be foraged from clean, unsplayed areas but can also be bought in garden centres or online from retailers such as Farmdrop in the UK and Marx Foods in the US.

INDEX

A

ale, caramelized onion & thyme soup 117
asparagus: fresh silky seasonal asparagus soup 19
  watercress & asparagus soup 36

B

bacon: Puy lentil & bacon soup 90
beans: black bean & tomato soup 110
  Cajun-style quinoa soup 71
  chunky Provençal vegetable & bean soup 78
  cream of celeriac & white bean soup 15
beef: beef goulash soup 98
  beef stock 9
  root vegetable & ground beef soup 86
  Vietnamese beef pho 105
beetroot & parsnip soup 35
bisque, lobster 129
black bean & tomato soup 110
bread: Comté croutes 67
  garlic croutons 12
  rarebit toast fingers 16
bream: Cambodian rice noodle & fish soup 55
broad/fava beans: watercress & asparagus soup 36
broccoli: purple sprouting broccoli soup 20
butter/lima beans: chunky Provençal vegetable & bean soup 78
butternut squash: carrot & butternut soup 39

carrot & fennel soup 23
winter squash soup 121

C D

Cajun-style quinoa soup 71
callaloo with sorrel & crab 126
Cambodian rice noodle & fish soup 55
cannellini beans: cream of celeriac & white bean soup 15
carrots: carrot & butternut soup 39
  carrot & fennel soup 23
cauliflower soup with coconut milk 43
celeriac/celery root: cream of celeriac & white bean soup 15
celery: pear, celery & blue cheese soup 31
cheese: Comté croutes 67
  pear, celery & blue cheese soup 31
  purple sprouting broccoli soup with blue cheese 20
  rarebit toast fingers 16
chia seed cream 110
chicken: chicken stock 9
  Chinese chicken soup 72
  game consommé 114
  gently spiced chicken & vegetable soup 93
  Goan chicken soup 97
  Malaysian chicken laksa 94
  spring vegetable & chicken broth 48
chickpeas/garbanzo beans: Moroccan harira 106
  summer minestrone 68
chillies/chiles: Thai pesto 85
Chinese chicken soup 72
chowder, New England clam 101

citrus broth with king prawns, chilli & ginger 122
clam chowder, New England 101
coconut milk: cauliflower soup with coconut milk 43
  creamy coconut & lamb soup 137
  sweet potato & coconut soup 85
consommé, game 114
corn-on-the-cob: summer corn soup 59
courgettes/zucchini: fennel & courgette soup 32
  green detox soup 75
  lettuce & courgette soup 64
crab: callaloo with sorrel & crab 126
croutes, Comté 67
croutons, garlic 12
Dashi broth with udon noodles & silken tofu 52
duck: dim sum duck wonton soup 138

E F

eggs: wild garlic & nettle soup 141
fava beans see broad beans
fennel: carrot & fennel soup 23
  fennel & courgette soup 32
field mushroom soup 40
fish: Cambodian rice noodle & fish soup 55
  fish stock 8
  mussel & fish soup 130
French onion soup 67

G H

game consommé 114
garbanzo beans see chickpeas

garlic croutons 12
gazpacho, Thai-style tomato 60
Goan chicken soup 97
goulash soup 98
green beans: miso soup with mushrooms & green beans 56
green detox soup 75
green tomato & sorrel soup 24
guinea fowl risotto soup 134
ham: creamy leek & potato soup 28
  London particular 109
harira, Moroccan 106
hazelnuts: cream of celeriac & white bean soup 15

I K

Istrian minestrone with pearl barley 102
kale: Cajun-style quinoa soup 71
kombu noodle broth 51

L

laksa, Malaysian chicken 94
lamb: creamy coconut & lamb soup 137
  Moroccan harira 106
leeks: creamy leek & potato soup 28
lemongrass paste 55
lentils: Moroccan harira 106
  Puy lentil & bacon soup 90
  velvety pumpkin & red lentil soup 81
lettuce & courgette soup 64
lima beans see butter beans
lobster bisque 129
London particular 109

M
Malaysian chicken laksa 94
minestrone: easy
minestrone with
spaghetti 89
Istrian minestrone with
pearl barley 102
summer minestrone 68
miso soup with
mushrooms & green
beans 56
Moroccan harira 106
mushrooms: Dashi broth
with udon noodles &
silken tofu 52
field mushroom soup 40
guinea fowl risotto soup
134
miso soup with
mushrooms & green
beans 56
mushroom soup 12
pheasant soup 133
Thai mushroom &
lemongrass broth 63
mussel & fish soup 130

N
nettles: wild garlic &
nettle soup 141
New England clam
chowder 101
noodles: Cambodian rice
noodle & fish
soup 55
Dashi broth with udon
noodles & silken tofu
52
kombu noodle broth 51
Malaysian chicken laksa
94
ramen bowls with
tempura prawns 125
Vietnamese beef pho
105

O P
onions: ale, caramelized
onion & thyme soup 117
French onion soup 67

pancetta: New England
clam chowder 101
watercress soup with
nashi pear, scallops &
pancetta 118
parsnips: beetroot &
parsnip soup 35
peanuts: Thai pesto 85
pears: pear, celery & blue
cheese soup 31
watercress soup with
nashi pear, scallops &
pancetta 118
pearl barley, Istrian
minestrone with 102
peas, dried: London
particular 109
peppers (bell): beef
goulash soup 98
gently spiced chicken &
vegetable soup 93
red pepper tapenade 59
tomato, red pepper &
sweet potato soup 44
pesto, Thai 85
pheasant soup 133
pho, Vietnamese beef 105
potatoes: creamy leek &
potato soup 28
fresh silky seasonal
asparagus soup 19
prawns: citrus broth with
king prawns, chilli &
ginger 122
ramen bowls with
tempura prawns 125
Provençal vegetable &
bean soup 78
pumpkin: velvety
pumpkin & red lentil
soup 81
purple sprouting broccoli
soup 20
Puy lentil & bacon soup 90

Q R
quinoa soup, Cajun-style
71
raita 137
ramen bowls with

tempura prawns 125
wild garlic *see* wild garlic
rarebit toast fingers 16
ratatouille soup 82
red kidney beans: Cajun-
style quinoa soup 71
red mullet: mussel & fish
soup 130
rice: Chinese chicken
soup 72
guinea fowl risotto soup
134
root vegetable & ground
beef soup 86
rouille 130

S
scallops: watercress soup
with nashi pear, scallops
& pancetta 118
sorrel: callaloo with sorrel
& crab 126
green tomato & sorrel
soup 24
spaghetti, easy
minestrone with 89
spinach soup with slow-
roasted tomatoes 27
spring vegetable &
chicken broth 48
stock 8–9
summer corn soup 59
summer minestrone 68
sweet potatoes: sweet
potato & coconut soup
85
tomato, red pepper &
sweet potato soup 44
sweetcorn: summer corn
soup 59

T
tapenade, red pepper 59
tempura prawns 125
tempura vegetables 51
Thai mushroom &
lemongrass broth 63
Thai pesto 85
Thai-style tomato
gazpacho 60

toast fingers, rarebit 16
tofu: Dashi broth with
udon noodles & silken
tofu 52
tomatoes: black bean &
tomato soup 110
fresh spinach soup with
slow-roasted
tomatoes 27
green tomato & sorrel
soup 24
roasted tomato soup 16
Thai-style tomato
gazpacho 60
tomato, red pepper &
sweet potato soup 44

V
vegetables: chunky
Provençal vegetable &
bean soup 78
easy minestrone with
spaghetti 89
Istrian minestrone with
pearl barley 102
ratatouille soup 82
root vegetable &
ground beef soup 86
spring vegetable &
chicken broth 48
tempura vegetables 51
vegetable stock 8
velvety pumpkin & red
lentil soup 81
Vietnamese beef pho 105

W Z
walnuts, salted sugared 31
watercress: watercress &
asparagus soup 36
watercress soup with
nashi pear, scallops &
pancetta 118
wild garlic/ramps & nettle
soup 141
winter squash soup 121
wonton soup, dim sum
duck 138
zucchini *see* courgettes

CREDITS

PHOTOGRAPHY

Peter Cassidy Pages 16, 24, 25, 61, 96, 100

Richard Jung Pages 17, 58, 69, 84

David Munns Page 102

Steve Painter Jkt back, pages 4, 6–11, 14, 18–22, 26, 29–31, 33–41, 46–49, 65, 76–79, 83, 87–89, 91, 92, 113–120, 123, 127–136, 140

William Reavell Spine, pages 2–3, 27, 32, 50, 80, 103, 106–108

Nassima Rothacker Jkt front, pages 66, 99

Toby Scott Page 137

Yuki Sugiura Pages 1, 112

Ian Wallace Pages 52–54, 95, 104, 124, 139

Kate Whitaker Pages 45, 63, 121, 144

Clare Winfield Pages 5, 13, 42, 56, 57, 59, 62, 70–75, 85, 90, 97, 110, 111, 122, 141

Endpaper photography all by Richard Jung, except sprouting broccoli and parsnips (by Steve Painter) and courgettes (by Debi Treloar)

RECIPES

Jordan Bourke
Tomato, red pepper & sweet potato soup with basil oil and vegetable crisps

Ross Dobson
Roasted tomato soup with rarebit toasts
Summer corn soup with red pepper tapenade
Summer minestrone with chickpeas & Pecorino
Sweet potato & coconut soup with Thai pesto

Amy Ruth Finegold
Black bean & tomato soup with lime & chia seed cream
Cajun-style quinoa soup with red beans & kale
Cauliflower soup with coconut milk
Chinese chicken soup with black forbidden rice
Green detox soup with hemp seeds

Mat Follas
Wild garlic & nettle soup with a poached egg

Dunja Gulin
Istrian minestrone with pearl barley
Kombu noodle broth with tempura vegetables
Velvety pumpkin & red lentil soup with turmeric

Vicky Jones
London Particular
Moroccan harira

Lizzie Kamenetzky
Beef goulash soup with sour cream

French onion soup with Comté croutes

Jenny Linford
Green tomato & sorrel soup
Miso soup with mushrooms & green beans
Mushroom soup with garlic croutons
Thai mushroom & lemongrass broth
Thai-style tomato gazpacho

Elsa Petersen-Schepelern
New England clam chowder
Goan chicken soup with spiced tarka

Louise Pickford
Cambodian rice noodle and fish soup
Dashi broth with udon noodles & silken tofu
Dim sum duck wonton soup
Malaysian chicken laksa
Ramen bowls with tempura prawns
Vietnamese beef pho

Belinda Williams
Ale, caramelized onion & thyme soup
Beef stock
Beetroot & parsnip soup with horseradish
Callaloo with sorrel & crab
Carrot & butternut soup with orange & ginger
Carrot & fennel soup with fresh lemon, dill & nigella seed
Chicken stock
Chunky Provençal vegetable & bean soup with smoked paprika
Citrus broth with king prawns, chilli & ginger
Cream of celeriac & white bean soup with toasted

hazelnuts & truffle oil
Creamy coconut & lamb soup with cumin, cardamom & almonds
Creamy leek & potato soup with ham hock
Easy minestrone with spaghetti
Fennel & courgette soup with Parmesan & crème fraîche
Field mushroom soup with Parmesan, thyme & pancetta
Fish stock
Fresh silky seasonal asparagus soup with sour cream & chives
Fresh spinach soup with slow-roasted tomatoes
Game consommé with softly boiled quails' eggs & brioche
Gently spiced chicken & vegetable soup with coconut & ginger
Guinea fowl risotto soup with porcini mushrooms, pumpkin & thyme
Lettuce & courgette/zucchini soup with chervil
Lobster bisque
Mussel & fish soup with rouille
Pear, celery & blue cheese soup with salted sugared walnuts
Pheasant soup with mushrooms & port
Purple sprouting broccoli soup with blue cheese
Puy lentil & bacon soup with seasonal greens
Ratatouille soup with goats' cheese, black olives & basil
Root vegetable & ground beef soup
Spring vegetable & chicken broth with kaffir lime & green herbs
Vegetable stock
Watercress & asparagus soup with baby broad beans
Watercress soup with nashi pear, scallops & pancetta
Winter squash soup with cep mushrooms & truffle oil